CLASSICAL COMICS
TEACHING RESOURCE PACK

Making Shakespeare accessible for teachers and students

Suitable for teaching ages 10–17

Written by: Karen Wenborn

William Shakespeare

CLASSICAL COMICS
TEACHING RESOURCE PACK

Macbeth

First printed: July 2009
Reprinted: November 2010

Published by: Classical Comics Ltd

Written by: Karen Wenborn
Character Designs & Original Artwork: Jon Haward
Colouring: Nigel Dobbyn
Inking Assistant: Gary Erskine
Design & Layout: Jo Wheeler & Carl Andrews
Editor in Chief: Clive Bryant

The rights of Jon Haward, Nigel Dobbyn and Gary Erskine
to be identified as the artists of this work have been asserted
in accordance with the Copyright, Designs and Patents Act
1988 sections 77 and 78.

Acknowledgments: Every effort has been made to trace
copyright holders of material reproduced in this book. Any rights
not acknowledged here will be acknowledged in subsequent
editions if notice is given to Classical Comics Ltd.

All enquiries should be addressed to:
Classical Comics Ltd.
PO Box 7280
Litchborough
Towcester
NN12 9AR, UK
Tel: 0845 812 3000

education@classicalcomics.com
www.classicalcomics.com

ISBN: 978-1-907127-01-4

Printed in the UK

CONTENTS

INTRODUCTION

WELCOME TO THE *MACBETH* TEACHING RESOURCE FROM CLASSICAL COMICS.

As always with our teaching resources we aim to provide enough information to satisfy teachers and students alike, in the form of enjoyable activities that children will engage with. The exercises are designed for teaching ages 10 - 17. They can be adapted to suit the needs of your classroom and customised to meet most skill levels. Our focus is, as always, on fun as well as learning.

This resource can be used alongside the Classical Comics adaptation as well as a traditional text, although that definitely isn't a requirement. In fact, many of the activities can stand on their own as introductions to the world of Shakespeare.

This Teaching Resource Pack provides cross curriculum topics and the opportunity to tailor lessons to meet individual needs. Together with the Classical Comics pioneering multi-text versions of the play, these resources provide differentiated teaching for all classrooms from ages 10 upward. The teaching resource provides exercises covering structure, listening, understanding, motivation and comprehension as well as key words, themes and literary techniques.

Many of the activities look at Shakespeare's use of language, but you will also see many applications within history, ICT, drama, reading, speaking, writing and art.

If you would like to provide feedback that will enhance this book, please email education@classicalcomics.com or visit www.classicalcomics.com. Your thoughts and input are always appreciated.

Karen Wenborn

**"Welcome hither:
I have begun to plant thee, and will labour
To make thee full of growing"**

SHAKESPEARE TIMELINE

Approx. Dates	Plays	What happened at the time?
1564		William Shakespeare was born in Stratford-Upon-Avon on 23rd April.
1572		Shakespeare possibly started at the New King's School grammar school in Stratford.
1582		Shakespeare married Ann Hathaway. By 1585 they had 3 children.
1586 - 1592	Maybe Shakespeare started writing his poetry here. No one knows when he did them. By 1601 he had written these poems: *VENUS AND ADONIS* *THE RAPE OF LUCRECE* *SONNETS* *A LOVER'S COMPLAINT* *THE PHOENIX AND THE TURTLE*	Nobody knows! Some people think that he travelled abroad, or that he was a teacher, or that he ran away from Stratford because he was in trouble for stealing a deer! He may have been one of "The Queen's Men" group of actors. In 1592 the playwright Robert Greene called Shakespeare an "upstart crow". He was jealous of the brilliant new writer!
1593		Shakespeare's friend and fellow playwright Christopher Marlowe is killed in a tavern in Deptford. All the theatres were shut because of the plague.
Before 1594	*HENRY VI* (three parts) *RICHARD III* *TITUS ANDRONICUS* *LOVE'S LABOURS LOST* *THE TWO GENTLEMEN OF VERONA* *THE COMEDY OF ERRORS* *THE TAMING OF THE SHREW*	Shakespeare joined "The Lord Chamberlain's Men" company of actors when the theatres reopened.
1594 - 1597	*ROMEO AND JULIET* *A MIDSUMMER NIGHT'S DREAM* *RICHARD II* *KING JOHN* *THE MERCHANT OF VENICE*	About this time, we think that Shakespeare wrote *LOVE'S LABOURS WON*, but the play has been lost!
1597 - 1600	*HENRY IV part i* *HENRY IV part ii* *HENRY V* *MUCH ADO ABOUT NOTHING* *MERRY WIVES OF WINDSOR* *AS YOU LIKE IT* *JULIUS CAESAR* *TROILUS AND CRESSIDA*	In 1597, Shakespeare bought a house in Stratford. In 1598, The Theatre in London burned down. In 1599, just after he finished *Henry V*, Shakespeare's company had The Theatre rebuilt as The Globe.
1601 - 1608	*HAMLET* *TWELFTH NIGHT* *MEASURE FOR MEASURE* *ALL'S WELL THAT ENDS WELL* *OTHELLO* *KING LEAR* *MACBETH* *TIMON OF ATHENS* *ANTONY AND CLEOPATRA* *CORIOLANUS*	Queen Elizabeth I died in 1603. James VI became James I of England and Wales. King James became the patron of Shakespeare's company "The King's Men", which means he had Royal support. In 1605, Guy Fawkes tried to blow up Parliament.
After 1608	*PERICLES* *CYMBELINE* *THE WINTER'S TALE* *THE TEMPEST* *HENRY VIII*	In 1613, The Globe burned down, then was rebuilt in 1614. Shakespeare retired to Stratford and did some writing with John Fletcher, his successor in "The King's Men". He died in 1616. In 1623, his plays were published in the *First Folio*.

WILLIAM SHAKESPEARE C.1564 – 1616

Shakespeare is, without question, the world's most famous playwright. Yet, despite his fame, very few records and artefacts exist for him today. We don't even know the exact date of his birth! Traditionally, however, April 23rd 1564 (St George's Day) is taken to be his birthday, as this was three days before his baptism (for which we do have a record). Records also tell us that he died on the same date in 1616, aged fifty-two.

The life of William Shakespeare can be divided into three acts.

Act One – Stratford-upon-Avon

William was the eldest son of tradesman John Shakespeare and Mary Arden, and the third of eight children (he had two older sisters). The Shakespeares were a respectable family. John made gloves and traded leather. The year after William was born, John became an alderman of Stratford-upon-Avon, and four years later he became High Bailiff (or mayor) of the town. Plague and illnesses were common in sixteenth-century England. The Bubonic Plague took the lives of many and was believed to have been the cause of death for three of William's seven siblings.

Little is known of William's childhood. He learnt to read and write at the local primary school, and later he is believed to have attended the local grammar school where he studied Latin and English Literature. In 1582, aged eighteen, William married a local farmer's daughter, Anne Hathaway. Anne was eight years his senior and three months pregnant. During their marriage they had three children: Susanna, born on May 26th 1583 and twins, Hamnet and Judith, born on February 2nd 1585. Hamnet, William's only son, died in 1596, aged eleven, from Bubonic Plague. Interestingly, the play *Hamlet* was written four years later.

Act Two – London

Five years into his marriage, in 1587, William's wife and children stayed in Stratford, while he moved to London. He appeared as an actor at 'The Theatre' (England's first permanent theatre), and gave public recitals of his own poems; but he quickly became famous for his playwriting. His fame soon spread far and wide. When Queen Elizabeth I died in 1603, the new King James I (who was already King James VI of Scotland) gave royal consent for Shakespeare's acting company, "The Lord Chamberlain's Men" to be called "The King's Men" in return for entertaining the court. This association was to shape a number of plays, such as *Macbeth*, which was written to please the Scottish King.

In just twenty-three years, between 1590 and 1613, William Shakespeare is attributed with writing and collaborating on 38 plays, 154 sonnets and 5 poems. No original manuscript exists for any of his plays, making it hard to accurately date them. Printing was still in its infancy, and plays tended to change as they were performed. Shakespeare would write manuscript for the actors and continue to refine them over a number of performances. The plays we know today have survived from written copies taken at various stages of each play and usually written by the actors from memory. This has given rise to variations in texts of what is now known as "quarto" versions of the plays, until we reach the first official printing of each play in the 1623 "folio" *Mr William Shakespeare's Comedies, Histories, & Tragedies*.

In 1599, Shakespeare and his troupe built 'The Globe Theatre' (using timbers from 'The Theatre' which they carried by boat across the River Thames!). This theatre, made even more famous today because of the New Globe Theatre on London's south bank, became the home of Shakespeare's plays, with thousands of people crammed into the small space for each performance. This lasted until 1613, when a cannon-shot during a performance of *Henry VIII* set fire to the thatched roof and the entire theatre was burnt to the ground. Although it was rebuilt a year later, it marked an end to Shakespeare's writing and to his time in London.

Act Three - Retirement

Shakespeare returned to live with his family in Stratford-upon-Avon. His last documented visit to London was in 1614 – a business trip with his son-in-law John Hall. He died on April 23rd 1616 and was buried two days later at the Church of the Holy Trinity (the same church where he had been baptised fifty-two years earlier). The cause of his death remains unknown.

His gravestone bears these words, believed to have been written by William himself:-

> *Good friend for Jesus sake forbear*
> *To dig the dust enclosed here.*
> *Blest be the man that spares these stones,*
> *And curst be he that moves my bones.*

Epilogue

At the time of his death, William Shakespeare had substantial properties, which he bestowed on his family and associates from the theatre. He had no son to inherit his wealth, and the fact that he wrote his second will in March 1616 displays an awareness of his likely death. His signature on that will is very shaky. The bulk of his will, including his substantial home, was left to his eldest daughter Susanna. Susanna's husband, John Hall, was the executor of the will. To his other daughter, Judith, he left money and possessions. Curiously, the only thing that he left to his wife Anne was his second-best bed! (although she continued to live in the family home after his death). William Shakespeare's last direct descendant died in 1670. She was his granddaughter, Elizabeth.

TO BE, OR NOT TO BE – THAT IS THE QUESTION	True or False?
1. Shakespeare was born in Stratford-upon-Avon in 1564	
2. His life and times are well documented	
3. Shakespeare's family were very poor	
4. He never went to school	
5. William Shakespeare married Anne Hathaway	
6. The whole Shakespeare family moved to London in 1587	
7. Shakespeare's group of actors performed his plays for King James I	
8. Shakespeare died in London	
9. Shakespeare was buried in Stratford-upon-Avon in 1616	
10. Descendants of Shakespeare are still alive today	

WILLIAM SHAKESPEARE C.1564 – 1616
A (VERY) BRIEF BIOGRAPHY

Despite his fame, few records exist for the life of William Shakespeare. He was born in Stratford-upon-Avon, we believe on April 23rd 1564. William was the eldest son of a respectable and reasonably affluent family. His father, John, was a local tradesman who went on to become the mayor of the town.

William learnt to read and write at the local primary school, and later he is believed to have attended grammar school. When he was 18, he married a local farmer's daughter, Anne Hathaway. They had three children together.

Five years later, the family stayed in Stratford while he moved to London. He appeared as an actor and gave public recitals of his own poems; but he quickly became famous for his playwriting. His fame soon spread far and wide. When Queen Elizabeth I died in 1603, the new King James I (who was already King James VI of Scotland) gave royal consent for Shakespeare's acting company to be called "The King's Men" in return for entertaining the court. This association was to shape a number of plays, such as *Macbeth*, which was written to please the Scottish King.

Between around 1590 and 1613, William Shakespeare is attributed with writing and collaborating on 38 plays, 154 sonnets and 5 poems. No original manuscript exists for any of his plays, making it hard to accurately date them and impossible to decide upon a definitive version

In 1599, Shakespeare and his troupe built 'The Globe Theatre'. This theatre became the home of Shakespeare's plays, with thousands of people crammed into the small space for each performance. In 1613, a cannon-shot during a performance of *Henry VIII* in 1613, set fire to the thatched roof and the entire theatre was burnt to the ground. Although it was rebuilt a year later, it marked an end to Shakespeare's writing and his time in London.

Shakespeare returned to Stratford-upon-Avon and died on April 23rd 1616, aged fifty-two. The cause of his death remains unknown. William Shakespeare's last direct descendant (his granddaughter, Elizabeth) died childless in 1670.

TO BE, OR NOT TO BE – THAT IS THE QUESTION	True or False?
1. Shakespeare was born in Stratford-upon-Avon in 1564	
2. His life and times are well documented	
3. Shakespeare's family were very poor	
4. He never went to school	
5. William Shakespeare married Anne Hathaway	
6. The whole Shakespeare family moved to London in 1587	
7. Shakespeare's group of actors performed his plays for King James I	
8. Shakespeare died in London	
9. Shakespeare was buried in Stratford-upon-Avon in 1616	
10. Descendants of Shakespeare are still alive today	

THE GLOBE THEATRE

**"All the world's a stage,
And all the men and women merely players"**

The first proper theatre in England was called The Theatre. Owned by James Burbage, it was built at Shoreditch, London in 1576. Before this playhouse was built, plays were performed outside inns or sometimes in the houses of rich people. Imagine seeing a play in a pub car park or in your sitting room! The Theatre was a big success and the Rose Theatre (1587) and the Hope Theatre (1613) followed. When The Theatre burned down in 1599, The Globe Theatre was built by Shakespeare's acting company in Southwark, London.

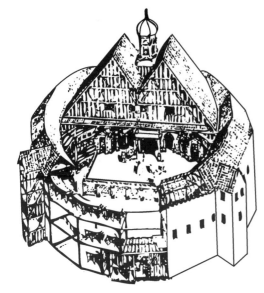

The Globe was the most magnificent theatre ever seen in London. It could hold thousands of people and didn't just show plays. It is rumoured that it was also a gambling house!

Plays were very popular and there was money to be made. Theatres would compete with each other and there was a constant demand for new material. As soon as a play was written, it was printed and put on stage straight away. Theatres would steal each other's ideas all the time. In fact, theatres were so popular that a law was introduced in 1591 to close them on a Thursday so that bull and bear baiting could still go on! Shakespeare could barely keep up, so sometimes the actors only had parts of the script to work from, called 'foul papers'. They often didn't even know what parts they were playing until the day of the performance and they would have to perform ten different plays in a week. There were no female actors. Only men were allowed to act, so all female parts had to be played by men. Two of the most famous actors at the time were Edward Alleyn and Will Kempe, who became very rich by investing in the theatre company The Admiral's Men.

When a play was about to start, the grounds surrounding the Globe Theatre would have been bustling with people. There would be market stalls outside and people would avoid work to go. The atmosphere would be like a football match today! The Latin motto of the Globe was "Totus mundus agit histrionem" (the whole world is a playhouse). Shakespeare used this in *As You Like It*, when he wrote the phrase "All the world's a stage".

The common people (called groundlings) would pay one penny to stand in the "pit" of the Globe. They had to put the money in a box as they went in. This is where we get the term "box office" from! The rich people would pay to sit comfortably in the galleries. Theatre performances were held in the afternoon, because no one had discovered electricity or gas yet to be able to light it inside at night. In 1593, 1603 and 1608 all theatres were closed due to the Bubonic Plague (The Black Death). This was probably when Shakespeare did most of his writing.

THE NEW GLOBE

Although the original Globe Theatre no longer exists, it is possible to now go and see a play in the same way that the Groundlings did in Shakespeare's day!

Shakespeare's Globe is a famous theatre that exists today in London at Bankside on the River Thames. It has been built using all of the information that could be found detailing the original, mostly from sketches of the time. You can turn a corner in London and suddenly imagine you are back in the 1500s.

An American actor and director called Sam Wanamaker decided years ago that there should be a permanent celebration of Shakespeare in London, so he started to get the Globe rebuilt. Work on the six metre deep foundations started in 1987 and the building was finally finished in 1997. Unfortunately, Sam died before it was finished but in 1993 the Queen honoured him with an honorary CBE for his hard work on the project.

GLOBE FACTS:

- As well as putting on plays, the new Globe provides Globe Education for schoolchildren, and the Globe Exhibition.
- Over 750,000 people go there each year!
- The site covers 21000 square metres!
- It has cost £30 million so far and they still want to spend £15 million on making it even better!
- The New Globe lies about 200 yards from what could be the remains of the original, which was found under a house in 1989!
- The Globe Theatre is 33ft high to the eaves (45ft overall).
- 6,000 bundles of Norfolk Water Reed were used on the Globe's roof.
- 36,000 handmade bricks were used.
- 90 tons of lime putty were used for the Tudor brickwork.
- 180 tons of lime plaster went into the outer walls.
- The Globe's pillars, which hold up the roof over the stage, are 28ft high and weigh 3 tons!

GLOBE RESEARCH SHEET 1

QUESTION: **Shakespeare's Globe, London**	
At Shakespeare's Globe in London, how many standing tickets are available for each performance?	
Who was the architect for Shakespeare's Globe?	
And the architect for the original Globe?	
Which play was performed at the original Globe in 1599?	
Write down 3 facts about The Globe.	
What is the Supporting Wall?	
Because of superstition, what name(s) for the play do actors use instead of *Macbeth*?	
Name three areas of the new Globe exhibition.	
Who was Edward Alleyn?	
In which other countries are there replicas of the Globe?	
In what year was *Macbeth* first performed?	

THE *OTHER* NEW GLOBE

The New Globe in London is so popular that they are building another one in America!

In 1812, the US and Britain were at war with each other. In New York Harbour, a military fort, Castle Williams, was built to defend the US against the British. It isn't there anymore but there are some remains that show it had the same shape as Shakespeare's Globe Theatre! Now, a new Globe is being built there to celebrate the culture that America and Britain have in common. They call it "The New Globe For The New World".

Foster and Partners

This new Globe project is supported by many famous actors and actresses, including Zoe Wanamaker, Sam Wanamaker's daughter!

The New Globe is being built on Governor's Island. In the 19th Century, a fort was built there but no shot was fired from there against the British.

It was then turned into a prison. Criminals were still locked up there well into the 20th century.

The courtyard is exactly the same shape as Shakespeare's Globe.

TASK:

Use the Internet to find out the answers to the questions on the **Globe Research Sheet.**

Find the information you need at:
www.newglobe.org
www.shakespeares-globe.org
www.bbc.co.uk

GLOBE RESEARCH SHEET 2

QUESTION: The New Globe, New York	ANSWER:
Name 3 of the actors who are supporting the project.	
Find the names of 3 other actors from the list that you have heard of and name a film play or TV show that they have been in. OR: If you haven't heard of any of them, find out what the 3 actors you have already named have been in.	
One of the actors who supports the project is Zoe Wanamaker. What is her connection to the Globe in London?	
BBC	
What BBC TV comedy features Zoe Wanamaker as the mother of a family? Who does she play in the Harry Potter films?	
In which *Doctor Who* episode did The Doctor and Martha meet William Shakespeare?	
In that episode, who played William Shakespeare?	
Write down 3 interesting facts about this episode of *Doctor Who*.	

THE GLOBE

GLOBE THEATRE: Label Descriptions

These are all jumbled up. Work out which description goes with which name, then label the diagram of The Globe with the information that you think is correct.

	Name	Description
1		The canopy over the stage, decorated with signs of the zodiac. There was a space above here from which actors could be lowered through a trapdoor as gods or angels.
2		Sometimes live music was played here but it was also used for acting as a wall or balcony.
3		There were trunks of oak trees put here to hold up The Heavens. The theatre was meant to be like the universe – divided into Heaven, Earth and Hell.
4		A thousand Groundlings would stand here to watch the plays. Noisy and smelly!
5		Here was the best place to sit if you were a lord or lady because everyone could see you – but your view might not be very good!
6		This led down to Hell! It was a room below the stage from where actors playing ghosts, witches and devils could make their entrance.
7		Rich playgoers could sit here on cushions.
8		An area behind the stage where costumes and props were kept and actors got changed.

Name	Number of description
The Heavens	
The Gentlemen's Rooms	
The Trapdoor	
The Yard	
The Musician's Gallery	
The Lord's Rooms	
The Tiring House	
The Pillars	

THE GLOBE

GLOBE THEATRE: Label Descriptions

Fill in the labels using the descriptions provided.

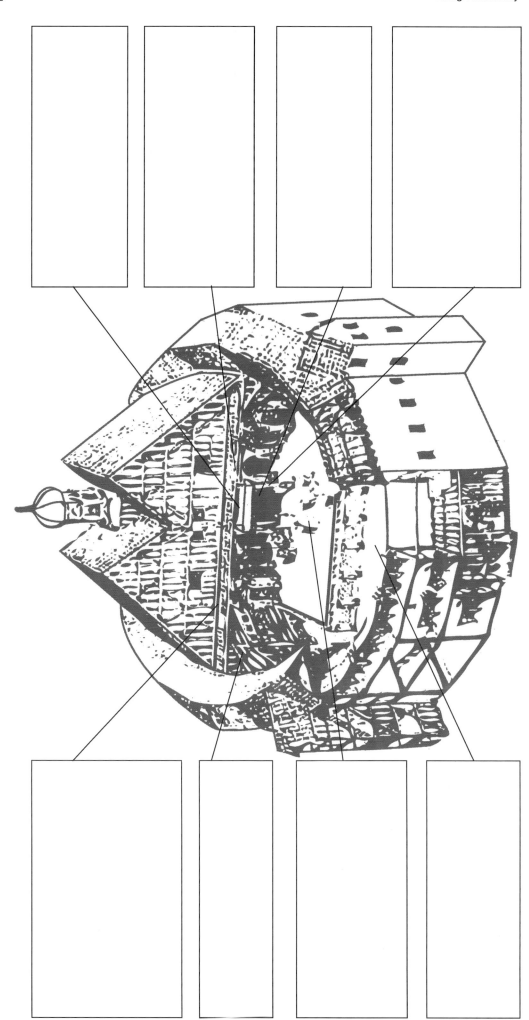

THE "SCOTTISH PLAY"

**"By the pricking of my thumbs,
Something wicked this way comes"**

Probably the most well known of all theatre superstition involves this play, *Macbeth* – more often called, by actors, "the Bards Play" or "the Scottish Play".

The superstition says that any company performing the play will be beset with the very worst of bad luck, ranging anywhere from a series of unexplained "accidents" on the set to deaths within the company! In fact, often it is not only the production of the play that will strike fear, but quoting from the play or even the mere mention of the name *Macbeth* inside a theatre, will be viewed askance by superstitious company members! Unless, of course, they are rehearsing the play at the time!

There are various theories about the origins of the "curse of Macbeth":

- The witches' incantations are said to be from real rituals and cast spells on the players
- During the play's first performance in 1606 legend has it that Hal Berridge, the boy playing Lady *Macbeth*, died backstage.
- When performed in Amsterdam in 1672, it is said that the actor playing Macbeth substituted a real dagger for the blunted stage one and with it killed the actor playing Duncan, in full view of the entranced audience.
- Because so many of the scenes take place in the dark, there tended to be a lot of accidents backstage.
- In the old days, whenever an acting company was in financial trouble, they would decide to perform *Macbeth* because it's a short play which usually pulls in the crowds. However, this wasn't always enough to save the theatre company. It was associated, therefore, with failure, hard times and being out of work. A constant worry for actors then and now.

TASKS

1. Break into groups and put together a list of superstitions that you know about or believe in.
2. Where do you think those superstitions came from? Why?
3. Do you know any "antidotes" to bad luck such as touching wood?
   List them and the superstitions they apply to.
4. Do you think we are more or less superstitious now than they were in Shakespeare's day?
   Explain why you think that.

Discuss with other groups. Do you all agree?

HISTORY OF THE PLAY

Although based on actual historical events, the story of *Macbeth* that we know today differs from what we believe to be true. There are two main reasons for this difference. Firstly, Shakespeare obtained his information from another book, which was itself inaccurate. Secondly, of course, Shakespeare needed to please his audience – and in particular the new King James I.

Holinshed

Raphael Holinshed's *Chronicles of England, Scotland and Ireland* was first published in 1574 and the second edition of 1587 was used by Shakespeare as a source for many of his historical plays. The following extract from *Chronicles* demonstrates just how closely he borrowed from Holinshed's version of events:

> "It fortuned as Makbeth and Banquho iournied towards Fores, where the king then laie, they went sporting by the waie together without other company saue onelie themselues, passing thorough the woods and fields, when suddenlie in the middest of a laund, there met them three women in strange and wild apparell, resembling creatures of the elder world, whome when they attentiuelie beheld, woondering much at the sight, the first of them spake and said: All haile Makbeth, thane of Glammis (for he had latelie entered into that dignitie and office by the death of his father Sinell). The second of them said: Haile Makbeth thane of Cawder. But the third said: All haile Makbeth that heereafter shalt be king of Scotland. Then Banquho: What manner of women (saith he) are you, that seeme so little fauourable vnto me, whereas to my fellow heere, besides high offices, ye assigne also the kingdome, appointing foorth nothing for me at all? Yes, (saith the first of them) we promise greater benefits vnto thee, than vnto him, for he shall reigne in deed, but with an vnluckie end: neither shall he leaue anie issue behind him to succeed in his place, where contrarilie thou in deed shalt not reigne at all, but of thee those shall be borne which shall gouern the Scotish kingdome by long order of continuall descent. Herewith the foresaid women vanished immediatlie out of their sight."

Although it wasn't Shakespeare's idea to introduce witches and fortune telling into the story, his brilliance lay in recognising an opportunity to not only create a spectacular masterpiece, but also please his very special audience.

King James I

Queen Elizabeth I died in 1603 and was succeeded by her cousin King James I (who was already King James VI in Scotland). He was a keen scholar and had a deep interest in witchcraft. He wrote a book on the subject which he called *Daemonologie* in 1597 and in it he advocated that witches should be dealt with severely. He was also a keen supporter of the arts, having the title of "The King's Men" bestowed upon Shakespeare's acting company soon after his coronation. In return for the title, The King's Men were expected to perform at court whenever they were asked, which amounted to around a dozen performances each year.

HISTORY OF THE PLAY

Macbeth is thought to have been written for performance in honour of a royal visit by the King of Denmark to King James I in 1606. It fits the requirement perfectly. Not only does it include strong elements of witchcraft to please King James I, but it also mentions the long line of Scottish Kings as well as displaying a harmonisation between England and Scotland.

It is with his portrayal of the witches where Shakespeare really aimed to please the King. In his own book, King James denounced witchcraft absolutely. It was his belief that witches were mostly women who had masculine features, typified by facial hair. They were in league with the devil, could summon up spirits, and could even curse images of people to control their destiny. King James believed that his right to be King was a God-given ruling – and the devil-based evil world of witchcraft was a threat to his divine right of kingship.

At the time it was written, the Stuart Kings of Scotland, which included King James, were believed to have descended from Banquo (this is unproven but may have some truth in it). The witches "predicted" a long line of kings and this is dealt with in the play verbally in Act 1 Scene III, and visually in Act IV Scene I when Macbeth is shown a large number of kings in a line, that all bear a resemblance to Banquo. The "bloodline" is only made possible by Fleance escaping when his father is attacked in Act III Scene III. Holinshed wrote how Walter Steward, the founder of the Stuart royal family (and who married the daughter of Robert Bruce) was a descendent of Fleance and therefore Banquo. This ancestral connection must have been behind a change that Shakespeare made to Holinshed's version of events. Holinshed had Banquo as an accomplice to Macbeth in Duncan's murder; but to show an ancestor of King James to have acted unlawfully would have been a rather foolish thing for Shakespeare to do!

The play shows the English and the Scots joining forces to overthrow Macbeth and restore Malcolm rightfully to the throne. This reflected the joint monarchy that King James brought to England and Scotland and there was much hope for peace between the two countries. Other pandering includes the reference to the English King (Edward the Confessor) having God-given powers to cure "the evil" in Act IV Scene III. King Edward was believed to have that power, and King James I revived the custom of sufferers being "touched" by the monarch as a cure.

Regardless of Shakespeare's motivation to write a play that would please his King, his first priority appeared to be his intention to create a masterpiece – and to this day *Macbeth* remains one of the brightest jewels in Shakespeare's worthy crown.

SHAKESPEARE'S SOURCE

Like many of Shakespeare's plays, Macbeth is not an original story. It is based on historical fact and Shakespeare used a popular history book of the day as a source for his information. The book, Chronicles of England, Scotland and Ireland, was written by Raphael Holinshed and published in 1574. Shakespeare used the second edition of the book, which appeared in 1587. The book was written in the language of the day which, along with the font used then, makes it look familiar, yet peculiar to modern readers. Often, Us and Vs were interchanged, as were Is and Js; also we spell some words differently today.

TASK:

Fill in the blanks
The unusual words have been blanked out, and appear in the original form in square brackets after the blank. Fill in the blanks with the correct word – as a guide we've done the first two for you:

"It fortuned as Macbeth [Makbeth] and Banquo [Banquho] _____ [iournied] towards

_____ [Fores], where the king then _____ [laie], they went sporting by the _____ [waie]

together without other company _____ [saue] _____ [onelie] _____ [themselues],

passing thorough the woods and fields, when _____ [suddenlie] in the _____

[middest] of a _____ [laund], there met them three women in strange and wild _____

[apparell], resembling creatures of the elder world, _____ [whome] when they _____

[attentiuelie] beheld, _____ [woondering] much at the sight, the first of them

_____[spake] and said: All _____ [haile] _____ [Makbeth], thane of _____

[Glammis] (for he had _____ [latelie] entered into that _____ [dignitie] and office by the

death of his father Sinell). The second of them said: _____ [Haile] _____ [Makbeth]

thane of _____ [Cawder]. But the third said: All _____ [haile] _____ [Makbeth]

that _____ [heereafter] _____ [shalt] be king of Scotland. Then _____

[Banquho]: What manner of women (_____ [saith] he) are you, that _____ [seeme] so little

_____ [fauourable] _____ [vnto] me, whereas to my fellow _____ [heere], besides

high offices, _____ [ye] _____ [assigne] also the _____ [kingdome], appointing

_____ [foorth] nothing for me at all? Yes, (_____ [saith] the first of them) we promise

greater benefits _____ [vnto] thee, than _____ [vnto] him, for he shall _____

[reigne] in deed, but with an _____ [vnluckie] end: neither shall he _____ [leaue]

_____ [anie] issue behind him to succeed in his place, where _____ [contrarilie] thou

in deed _____ [shalt] not _____ [reigne] at all, but of thee those shall be borne which

shall _____ [gouern] the _____ [Scotish] _____ [kingdome] by long

order of _____ [continuall] descent. Herewith the foresaid women vanished

_____ [immediatlie] out of their sight."

WHEN WAS THAT?

When we think about a Shakespeare play we usually associate it closely with the Elizabethan era. Although his plays are regularly modernised, we expect to see the actors in the fashion of the day – tights, baggy shirts, ruffs, small capes, etc. Despite that, we are always struck by the complexity of his language and give no allowance that his wonderful words were written over 400 years ago! Life was very different in Shakespeare's day. The Globe Theatre, which is in the middle of London's busy city streets today, was in relative countryside back then; and things that we take for granted in modern times, such as printing and long distance travelling, were rare.

So just how different was life in Elizabethan England? To put it into context, here is a list of inventions and facilities. They are in no particular order. All you have to do is decide if they were around when Shakespeare began writing his plays (let's say 1590).

Invention	Around in 1590? (Y / N)	Century / date it was invented	Comments
Gunpowder			
Iron (the material, not the household appliance!)			
Steel			
Bronze			
Aeroplane (powered)			
Trebuchet / Catapult			
Longbow			
Motor car (not steam)			
Bicycle			

WHEN WAS THAT?

Invention	Around in 1590? (Y / N)	Century / date it was invented	Comments
Steam engine			
Purpose-built canals			
Steam locomotive			
Water pump			
Telescope			
Computer			
The wheel			
Telephone			
Biro / ball-point pen			
Mechanical printing press (to create books and posters)			

You get extra points if you put the century that each of these was introduced. Remember that centuries are "1 out" in that the 16th Century was from 1501 to 1600, the 17th Century from 1601 to 1700 and today we are in the 21st Century.

MAC BETHAD MAC FINDLÁECH

(1005 - 15 August 1057)

Known in English as Macbeth, Mac Bethad Mac Findláech was King of Scots (or Alba) from 1040 until his death in 1057. He is best known as the subject of William Shakespeare's tragedy *Macbeth* and although the play is often historically inaccurate, it has seeds of truth buried within it.

Macbeth was born to Findláech mac Ruaidrí, Mormaer of Moray (high steward, lord or ruler) in the north of Scotland, around 1005.

Macbeth's mother's name Donada, is unconfirmed, but she is variously said to have been the daughter of King Kenneth II or the daughter of King Malcolm II. Either of who as a grandfather would later help to cement his claim to the throne.

In 1020, Macbeth's father Findláech was killed, most probably by his brother Máel Brigté's son Máel Coluim and was succeeded by his nephew Gille Coemgáin. In 1032, Gille Coemgáin and fifty other people were burned to death in retribution for the murder of Findláech, probably by Macbeth and allies. Macbeth then succeeded his cousin Gille Coemgáin to become Mormaer of Moray in 1031.

At around the same time Macbeth married Gille Coemgáin's widow, Gruoch and became step-father to her son by Gille Coemgáin, Lulach. This marriage was significant, as Gruoch was the grand-daughter of Kenneth III, ensuring that, as a couple, the Macbeth's had a strong claim to the throne.

Duncan

When Duncan I took the Scottish throne, his grandfather Malcolm is likely to have had the blood of several relatives on his hands, as he may well have murdered the way clear for Duncan.

Given the circumstances, Duncan would have been wise to make peace with his remaining family, in particular his cousins Thorfinn the Mighty, Earl of Orkney, Macbeth, and the person closest to his throne in terms of lineage, Gruoch, later to be the wife of Macbeth.

Macbeth soon pressed his own claim to the throne with the help of that same cousin and ally, Earl Thorfinn of Orkney. He eventually won the crown by slaying Duncan at Bothgowanan near Elgin, Scotland in 1040.

Macbeth has been judged by history to be a better king than his predecessor. Under his rule Scotland became relatively stable and quite prosperous , so much so in fact, that by 1050 he was confident enough to leave the country for a number of months and make a pilgrimage to Rome! At this time he was said to have been so wealthy that he "scattered alms like seed corn".

In 1054, Duncan I's son, Malcolm Canmore, challenged Macbeth for the throne of Scotland in alliance with Siward, Earl of Northumbria (who, by the way, also happened to be Duncan's wife's cousin) and they took control of much of southern Scotland.

On 15 August 1057 Macbeth's army was finally defeated at the Battle of Lumphanan, in Aberdeenshire, and Macbeth was killed in battle. He was later buried in the graveyard at Saint Oran's Chapel on the Isle of Iona, the last of many Kings of Alba and Dalriada to be laid to rest there.

THE REAL MACBETH - TIMELINE

**"Upon my head they placed a fruitless crown,
And put a barren sceptre in my gripe,
Thence to be wrench'd with an unlineal hand,
No son of mine succeeding."**

Date	Key events during the reign of the real Macbeth
1020	Findláech, Macbeth's father was killed.
1031-2	Gille Coemgáin and fifty other people were burned to death in retribution for the murder of Findláech.
1031-2	Becomes Mormaer of Moray on the death of Gille Coemgáin. Marries Gruoch.
1040	Macbeth becomes king of Alba on the death of Duncan I.
1050	Macbeth makes a pilgrimage to Rome, Italy.
1054	Duncan I's son, Malcolm Canmore claims the throne.
1057	Macbeth's army was defeated at the Battle of Lumphanan in Aberdeenshire, Scotland, and Macbeth was killed.

ABOUT MACBETH:

BORN: 1005 (possibly).

PARENTS: Findláech and (possibly) Donada.

ASCENDED THE THRONE: 1040.

TITLES: Mormaer of Moray
King of Alba.

MARRIED: Gruoch. Widow of Gille Coemgáin and daughter of Biote (Beoedhe), who was in turn the son of King Kenneth III or Kenneth II.

CHILDREN: None known.

DIED: Battle of Lumphanan, 15 August 1057.

BURIED: Saint Oran's Chapel on the Isle of Iona, Scotland.

MACBETH - SHAKESPEARE'S STORY

It's 11th century Scotland. Macbeth, Thane of Glamis, is one of King Duncan's greatest war captains. Upon returning from a battle with the rebellious Thane of Cawdor, Macbeth and Banquo encounter three witches, who prophecy that Macbeth will become Thane of Cawdor and then King. They also prophecy that Banquo will become the father of kings. When Lady Macbeth hears this, she is determined to push her husband to take fate into his own hands and make himself king by murdering Duncan.

Macbeth is reluctant to harm Duncan. But, when the King makes arrangements to visit Macbeth's castle, the opportunity presents itself. Pressed on by his wife, Macbeth kills Duncan and blames the King's drunken attendants, who he also kills. However, Macbeth is racked with guilt and begins to see apparitions. When the body is discovered, Malcolm and Donalbain, the King's sons, are suspicious of Macbeth and flee for their lives. To everyone else, it looks as if the sons have been the chief conspirators and Macbeth is crowned King of Scotland.

Banquo's suspicions grow, based on his encounter with the witches and Macbeth is wary of the second prophecy concerning Banquo's offspring. Macbeth hires assassins to kill Banquo and his son, Fleance. Banquo is murdered that night, but Fleance escapes. The bloody ghost of Banquo appears to Macbeth at a feast, tormenting his already guilty conscience. In addition, Macduff, once a comrade of Macbeth, has fled after the King's sons to England, as he also suspects Macbeth. In revenge, Macbeth butchers Macduff's entire household.

Macduff and the King's sons raise an army in England and march against Macbeth, who is given another prophecy by the witches, as he prepares for the assault. They tell him his throne is safe until Birnam Wood comes to Dunsinane and he will not die by the hand of any man born of a woman.

Macbeth now feels invincible. Lady Macbeth, on the other hand, has been slowly driven mad by her dreams, in the wake of Duncan's murder. She sleepwalks and eventually kills herself. Macbeth learns that many of his lords are deserting and joining Malcolm's army, which approaches Dunsinane under cover of boughs, which they've cut from the trees of Birnam Wood.

Macbeth and Macduff eventually meet on the bloody battlefield. Macbeth laughs derisively, relating the witches' prophecy. But Macduff retorts that he was "from his mother's womb untimely ripp'd" and not (technically) "of woman born".

The play ends with the death of Macbeth and Malcolm being crowned King of Scotland.

MACBETH - SHAKESPEARE'S STORY

TEST YOURSELF

1. Who is with Macbeth when he meets the witches for the first time?

2. Who are the first three characters to die?

3. What is the second prophesy?

4. Who does Macbeth hire assassins to kill?

5. Who appears as a ghost at the feast?

6. Where does Macduff flee?

7. What is the third prophesy?

8. What happens to Lady Macbeth?

9. Who kills Macbeth?

10. At the end of the play, who becomes King?

MACBETH - SHAKESPEARE'S STORY

TASKS & ACTIVITIES:

Go online or use reference books to find out more and answer the questions.

What is the word we use to describe the murder of a King?

Can you find any other Kings in history that were murdered?

What can you find out about witches?

In 1597 an English King wrote a book about witches. Who was he?

Do you think this influenced Shakespeare's story of Macbeth?

How?

When was witchcraft made illegal in England?

What was the "castle" of Dunsinane really like? Draw a picture.

On paper or on a computer draw a map of Scotland showing all of the places mentioned in *Macbeth*.

What is the name of the witches' cat?

How did the people in Tudor times test to find out if someone was a witch?

How many prophesies did the witches make?

What were these prophesies?

MACBETH - SCENE BY SCENE SYNOPSIS

Act I Scene I

Three witches gather in a bleak, remote place and agree to meet with Macbeth.

Act I Scene II

At his camp near Forres, King Duncan receives an update about the battle that is taking place between his army and some rebels, led by Macdonwald. All of the reports commend the bravery of his captains Macbeth (the Thane of Glamis)

and Banquo. The second report from the Thane of Rosse tells the King about Macbeth's victory against a former ally of the King, the Thane of Cawdor. The King orders the Thane of Cawdor to be executed and for that title to be given to Macbeth.

Act I Scene III

On their way back to Forres from the battle, Macbeth and Banquo are greeted by the three witches, who prophesise that Macbeth will become the Thane of Cawdor, and eventually, King of Scotland. They also predict that Banquo will not be king, but will be the father of kings. Macbeth believes that the Thane of Cawdor is still alive, and therefore both captains dismiss the prophecies. However, the Thane of Rosse and the Thane of Angus meet Macbeth and tell him that he has indeed become the Thane of Cawdor, at the King's request. This makes him start to believe the words of the witches, and he begins to consider how he can make their prediction of kingship come true.

Act I Scene IV

At his palace at Forres, King Duncan greets Macbeth and Banquo, and thanks them heartily for their bravery. He also confirms to all present that his eldest son, Malcolm, will succeed him to the throne. King Duncan announces that they are to visit Macbeth's castle in Inverness, and so Macbeth leaves early to prepare for them.

MACBETH - SCENE BY SCENE SYNOPSIS

Act I Scene V
Macbeth's wife, Lady Macbeth, receives a letter from her husband telling her about the witches' prophecies. Her ambition makes her determined to be the driving force behind Macbeth becoming king and she realises that the only way that can happen is for King Duncan to be murdered. When she receives word of the King's visit to their Inverness home, she sees her opportunity to have Duncan killed and for her husband to become king. When Macbeth arrives at the castle, she resolves that King Duncan will not live to see the next day ("O! never shall sun that morrow see!").

Act I Scene VI
King Duncan arrives at Macbeth's castle, and receives a warm welcome from Lady Macbeth.

Act I Scene VII
While the banquet held in the King's honour is in full flow, Macbeth leaves the group to be alone with his thoughts. He is wrestling with his conscience about killing the very person that he should remain loyal to and that he has in the past fought to defend. ("If it were done, when 'tis done, then 'twere well it were done quickly"). Lady Macbeth finds him away from his guests and chastises him, not only for ignoring his duties as a host, but also for his lack of resolve towards committing the evil deed. Once more, she convinces him to kill Duncan ("But screw your courage to the sticking-place, and we'll not fail").

Act II Scene I
The banquet is over. Banquo and his son Fleance are restless, and are walking around inside the castle walls. They meet with Macbeth and briefly discuss the witches. When Banquo and Fleance leave Macbeth alone, he starts to hallucinate, seeing an imaginary dagger in front of him, leading him to the King's chamber ("Is this a dagger which I see before me"). The ringing of the bell signifies to Macbeth that he must go and kill the king.

Act II Scene II
Macbeth is full of remorse. Lady Macbeth is proud of her achievements and her cunning plan that has allowed the murder. She provides stiff resolve to Macbeth, and is critical of her husband's guilt, which she perceives as cowardice. Lady Macbeth ensures that the plan is followed to the letter, by placing the murder weapons by the side of the drunken guards (Macbeth refuses to re-enter the room). She dismisses the blood they have on their own hands, saying that it will easily wash off. A loud knocking at the castle gate interrupts them.

MACBETH - SCENE BY SCENE SYNOPSIS

Act II Scene III

The knocking signifies the arrival of Macduff (Thane of Fife) and the Thane of Lenox, who were told to visit the king there early in the morning. They are let in by the Porter, and shortly afterwards greeted by Macbeth who pretends that he has been woken by their arrival. Macduff goes to wake the king, while Lenox tells Macbeth of the eerie and terrible happenings that they'd encountered during the night just passed. Macduff bursts out of the King's chamber in shock ("O horror! horror! horror!"). Other guests from the night before quickly gather and they all learn that the king has been killed. Macbeth murders the guards, supposedly out of rage, before they have chance to wake up (and reveal the truth), while Lady Macbeth faints (although this is an act). Fearing for their own lives, Duncan's sons, Malcolm and Donalbain, flee to England and Ireland respectively.

Act II Scene IV

Outside the castle, an old man discusses the odd goings-on in nature during the night, with the Thane of Rosse (such as Duncan's horses eating each other). Macduff joins them, and they discuss how Macbeth will be crowned king at Scone. Rosse will be going to the ceremony, but Macduff is suspicious and decides to return to his home in Fife instead.

Act III Scene I

Macbeth is now king, but he is afraid of Banquo fathering children who will take his crown from him. Macbeth considers that he has committed his crime ultimately for the benefit of Banquo's children. Similarly, Banquo is suspicious of Macbeth's "good fortune". Macbeth finds out that Banquo is going out riding that evening, and arranges for him and his son to be murdered.

Act III Scene II

Lady Macbeth is aware that her husband is unhappy. They discuss their situation, trying to reassure each other that they did the right thing to engineer their status. Macbeth hints to Lady Macbeth that Banquo will be dealt with.

Act III Scene III

Three murderers carry out Macbeth's instructions, to kill Banquo and his son Fleance. Banquo is murdered, "Let it come down") but in the confusion, Fleance escapes with his life. The murderers decide to admit the truth to Macbeth, that only half of the job was done.

MACBETH - SCENE BY SCENE SYNOPSIS

Act III Scene IV

Macbeth invites all of the noblemen to a grand banquet. Just before it gets underway he receives news from one of the murderers that Banquo has been killed, and Fleance has fled. When he returns to the banquet, he is horrified to see the ghost of Banquo sitting in the only remaining chair. As no one else can see the ghost, his guests believe that he has lost his sanity. Lady Macbeth tries to cover up the actions of her husband, but to no avail – and the evening's festivities are brought to an abrupt end. Once the guests are gone, Macbeth explains what he has seen to his wife, who blames him for ruining the evening. He resolves to seek out the witches the next day for a full explanation and further prophesies.

Act III Scene V

Hecate, the "Queen of the witches" is angry that the three witches have interfered with the natural course of events, encouraging Macbeth to become king through foul means.

Act III Scene VI

The Thane of Lenox and another lord (whose identity is unknown) discuss the current situation. They express their dislike of Macbeth, calling him a tyrant; and agree that their hopes of having Scotland return to its former glory rest with Duncan's son Malcolm, who has gone to England to gather an army, with which he'll try to reclaim the throne.

Act IV Scene I

Macbeth goes to visit the witches, seeking more information. Through an elaborate spell, they conjure up images, apparitions and spirits; and through these Macbeth is led to understand a number of things. Firstly, that he should be wary of Macduff, the Thane of Fife. Secondly, that Macbeth cannot be harmed by anyone that was born of a woman, ("None of woman born shall harm Macbeth"). Thirdly, that Macbeth will not be defeated until Birnam Wood comes to Dunsinane. When Macbeth wants to know more, the witches conjure up a vision of a line of kings, which all look like Banquo. Suddenly, the visions and the witches disappear, and Macbeth is alone. The Thane of Lenox arrives and Macbeth instructs him to organise the murder of Macduff, his wife and their children.

Act IV Scene II

Lady Macduff is told by her cousin, the Thane of Rosse, that Macduff has gone to England, thus leaving her and her children alone. Shortly after Rosse leaves, murderers arrive at the castle, and savagely kill her and her family.

MACBETH - SCENE BY SCENE SYNOPSIS

Act IV Scene III

Malcolm and Macduff meet up in England. Malcolm is a little wary of Macduff, thinking that he could be a spy for Macbeth. Macduff of course is genuinely loyal to Malcolm and they soon decide to fight side-by-side against the tyrant Macbeth. The Thane of Rosse has the unenviable task of breaking the news to Macduff that his wife and all of his children have been murdered: action that was organised by Macbeth. This stiffens Macduff's resolve to take revenge on Macbeth, and it is organised that Malcolm shall lead an army comprising himself and Macduff, as well as ten thousand English soldiers led by Siward, the Earl of Northumberland.

Act V Scene I

One of the women who waits on Lady Macbeth calls for a doctor to witness the Queen sleepwalking. Not only do they see her pretending to wash her hands ("Out, damned spot") but they also hear her admit to her involvement in the murders of Duncan, Macduff's family, and Banquo.

Act V Scene II

Certain Scottish noblemen gather in preparation to meet the approaching English force, led by Malcolm, so that they can join forces with them at Birnam Wood.

Act V Scene III

Macbeth is preparing his defences at Dunsinane Castle. He receives further confirmation of Malcolm's advancing army. Although Macbeth is aware that some thanes are deserting him to join up with Malcolm, he remains defiant; relying on the information that any man that was born of a woman cannot hurt him and in any case, his reign will last until Birnam Wood comes to Dunsinane. Macbeth is more concerned about preparing for battle than discussing his wife's illness with the doctor.

Act V Scene IV

Having arrived at Birnam Wood, Malcolm instructs his soldiers to cut down branches and use them as camouflage so that they can mount a surprise attack on Macbeth.

MACBETH - SCENE BY SCENE SYNOPSIS

Act V Scene V

While preparing Dunsinane Castle for war, Macbeth hears a scream. It is confirmed to him that Lady Macbeth is dead. This shocks Macbeth out of his battle preparations to reveal his feelings towards her and a regret for how things have worked out ("She should have died hereafter"). But his grieving isn't allowed to last long. He is interrupted by a message that Birnam Wood is approaching Dunsinane (it looks like that because the soldiers are carrying branches). Naturally, Macbeth is dismayed at the materialisation of this seemingly impossible prophecy. However, he resolves to fight regardless of this and he orders his army to prepare for battle.

Act V Scene VI

When Malcolm's army reach the castle, he orders his men to throw down their camouflage. He instructs Siward to lead the attack on Dunsinane, leaving Malcolm and Macduff to follow behind as a second wave.

Act V Scene VII

As the battle rages, Siward's son comes across Macbeth. Bolstered by the belief of his own invincibility ("What's he, that was not born of woman? Such a one am I to fear, or none"), Macbeth kills Young Siward. Macduff searches for his enemy Macbeth on the battlefield, but cannot find him. Meanwhile, Dunsinane Castle is defeated, and Malcolm and Old Siward make claim to it.

Act V Scene VIII

Despite his army leaving him, Macbeth is determined to fight for his kingship. Macduff eventually tracks his enemy down and they fight each other. Macbeth still believes that he is invincible ("I bear a charmed life; which must not yield to one of woman born") until Macduff tells him that he was born by Caesarean Section, i.e. cut from his mother's womb rather than "being of woman born". Macbeth suddenly realises his own mortality and after a long fight, Macduff kills Macbeth.

Act V Scene IX

At Dunsinane Castle, Old Siward receives news that his son was killed in battle. Despite the loss, he is proud that his son died bravely (proved by him sustaining his wounds on the front of his body). When Macduff appears, holding the head of Macbeth, Malcolm is pronounced King of Scotland, and he goes on from there to be crowned at Scone.

FAMILY TREE

Look at the Family Tree on the next page and answer the questions below.

1. Was Malcolm II related to Macbeth?

2. Who was Gruoch's first husband?

3. What was the name of Gruoch's son?

4. Which royal 'house' did Macbeth belong to?

5. How were Grouch 1 and 2 connected?

6. Who succeeded Macbeth?

7. Which Malcolm took the throne in 1058?

Can you research and then draw the family tree of James VI of Scotland (James I of England) showing the unbroken Stuart lineage?

See how far you can go!

FAMILY TREE

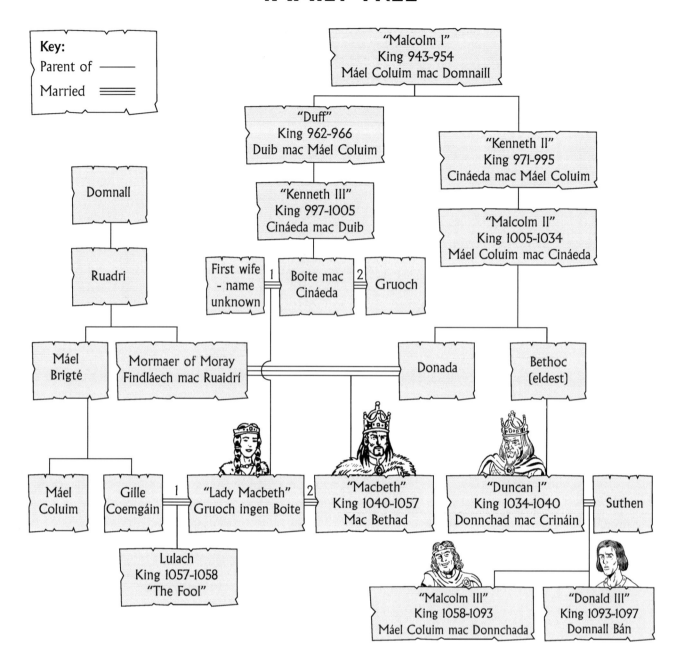

Key:
Parent of ———
Married ═══

The Macbeth Murder Trail

1020 – Macbeth's father Findláech died – thought to have been killed by his own nephew, Máel Coluim. His title of High Steward went to Máel Coluim's brother, Gille Coemgáin.

1032 – Gille Coemgáin and 50 other people were burned to death as punishment for the killing of Findláech. Thought to have been carried out by Macbeth and his allies as retribution for killing his father. Macbeth takes his title (that had been his father's) and also takes Gille Coemgáin's widow, Gruoch, for his wife.

There is another theory, that Gille Coemgáin killed Boite mac Cináeda because he had made his wife the heiress to his estate. As retaliation for this murder, Boite's wife Gruoch (the stepmother of the

Gruoch that married Gille Coemgáin and later Macbeth) mustered an army to kill Gille Coemgáin.

1040 – Macbeth killed King Duncan I at Bothgowanan.

1050 – Macbeth went on a pilgrimage to Rome.

1054 – Máel Coluim mac Donnchada (Malcolm, son of King Duncan I) stakes his claim to the throne and challenges Macbeth in the first of a series of battles.

1057 – Macbeth's army is finally defeated by Malcolm's army at the Battle of Lumphanan. Macbeth is killed in battle. Macbeth's step-son Lulach becomes King.

1057 – After only a few months of rule, Malcolm kills Lulach and becomes King Malcolm III of Scotland.

Please note: This family tree does not show every member of the families.

MONARCHS OF SCOTLAND

House of Alpin	House of Dunkeld	House of Stewart
Kenneth I (843-858)	Malcolm III (1058-1093)	Robert II (1371-1390)
Donald I (858-863)	Donald III/Edmund (1093-1097)	Robert III (1390-1406)
Constantine I (863-877)	Duncan II (1094)	James I (1403-1437)
Aedh (877-878)	Edgar (1097-1107)	James II (1437-1460)
Eochaid & Giric (878-889)	Alexander I (1107-1024)	James III (1460-1488)
Donald II (889-900)	David I (1124-1153)	James IV (1488-1513)
Constantine II (900-943)	Malcolm IV (1153-1165)	James V (1513-1542)
Malcolm I (943-954)	William I (1165-1214)	Mary I (1542-1567)
Indulf (954-966)	Alexander II (1214-1249)	James VI (1567-1625)
Duff (962-966)	Alexander III (1249-1286)	
Culen (966-971)	Margaret (1286-1290)	
Kenneth II (971-995)	The Bruces & The Balliols	
Constantine III (995-997)	(1292-1830)	
Kenneth III (997-1005)	John Balliol (1292-1296)	
Malcolm II (1005-1034)	Robert I (1306-1329)	
Duncan I (1034-1040)	David II (1329-1371)	
Macbeth (1040-1057)	Edward Balliol (1332-1356)	
Lulach (1057-1058)		

MACBETH

"If chance will have me king, why, chance may crown me."

From a brave, loyal subject to a murderous tyrant?
Macbeth is a man who at the start of the play appears to be a good man, with loyal friends, one who fights for his king. By the end of the play he has become someone of ruthless ambition and without a conscience.

How does that happen? How does Shakespeare demonstrate this in the play?

TASKS

1. Tell the story, in your own words, of Macbeth
    fighting against Macdonwald and the Norwegians.
    What was the King, Duncan's reaction?
    What did he think of Macbeth at this stage?

2. The witches gave the first prophesy to Macbeth and
    Banquo.
    What did they promise Macbeth?
    How did he react at the time?
    What had changed after he talked with Lady
    Macbeth?

3. "But in these cases,
    We still have judgment here; that we but teach
    Bloody instructions, which, being taught, return
    To plague th' inventor: this even-handed justice
    Commends th' ingredients of our poison'd chalice
    To our own lips.
    He's here in double trust;
    First, as I am his kinsman and his subject,
    Strong both against the deed; then, as his host,
    Who should against his murderer shut the door,
    Not bear the knife myself."
    (From Act I Scene I)

    Describe in your own words what Macbeth is
    feeling now.

4. Which scene in the play do you think demonstrates
    the fact that Macbeth no longer has the morals and
    restraints he began with?
    Describe the differences between Macbeth,
    Duncan's loyal servant at the start of the story, and
    Macbeth the King.
    Is Macbeth truly evil, or simply weak?

5. What are your views about Macbeth at the end of
    the play?

LADY MACBETH

**"Had he not resembled
My father as he slept, I had done't."**

Lady Macbeth appears to be an aggressive and ambitious character.
She also seems to be the key influence on Macbeth's behaviour. However, following the murder of
Duncan, Lady Macbeth's conscience becomes too great for her and her mental and physical condition
deteriorates to the point where she ends her own life.

DISCUSSION:

Debate the following within groups. Find quotes that back up your argument.

Would Lady Macbeth have killed Duncan if Macbeth had refused to act?

Does she end her life because of guilt? Or for other reasons?

Who do you think was the major influence on Macbeth?
Why?

Is Lady Macbeth more culpable than Macbeth for the murder of King Duncan?

Is Lady Macbeth a more evil character than her husband and, if so, why?

TASK

Imagine you are Lady Macbeth.
Write a diary of events from the first prophesy, to the day
after the banquet when Banquo appears as a ghost.

DUNCAN

**"Besides, this Duncan
Hath borne his faculties so meek, hath been
So clear in his great office, that his virtues
Will plead like angels, trumpet-tongued, against
The deep damnation of his taking-off;"**

QUESTIONS:
Write your answers on a separate sheet of paper.

Act I Scene I
1. Who is Duncan conferring with at the start of the play?
2. When Duncan says "O valiant cousin! worthy gentleman!" who is he talking about?

Act I Scene IV
3. Who has betrayed Duncan?
4. What does Duncan announce?
5. What does Duncan mean by this: -
    **"True, worthy Banquo: he is full so valiant
    And in his commendations I am fed;
    It is a banquet to me. Let's after him,
    Whose care is gone before to bid us welcome:
    It is a peerless kinsman."**
6. What is Macbeth thinking at this time?

Act I Scenes VI and VII
7. Who accompanies Duncan to Macbeth's castle?
8. Do you think Duncan suspects Macbeth? Explain your answer.
9. What does Macbeth mean by this speech?
    **"He's here in double trust;
    First, as I am his kinsman and his subject,
    Strong both against the deed; then, as his host,
    Who should against his murderer shut the door,
    Not bear the knife myself."**
10. Write this speech again using your own words.

BANQUO

**"Thou canst not say I did it; never shake
Thy gory locks at me."**

Banquo is a general in Duncan's army and Macbeth's friend. Together with Macbeth, Banquo helps Duncan's forces achieve victory over the king of Norway and the Thane of Cawdor. Following the battle, Banquo and Macbeth meet the witches, who make several prophesies about Macbeth and Banquo.

Shakespeare's Banquo appears to be the very opposite of Macbeth - his moral "good side". Banquo has no "vaulting ambition" and he escapes the trap of believing the witches' prophesies.

QUESTIONS
Write your answers on a separate sheet of paper.

1.   The witches tell Banquo that he will be the father of future kings. How does Banquo's reaction reveal his true character?

2.   Banquo expresses doubts about the witches and their prophecies. Give an example of a quote that illustrates this.

3.   What does Banquo do after Duncan's murder?

4.   Does Banquo realise that Macbeth has committed the murder?

5.   Why doesn't Banquo accuse Macbeth?

6.   What does Macbeth hope to gain from killing Banquo and Fleance?

7.   Why does Banquo haunt Macbeth? Explain Macbeth's reaction in your own words.

TASK
Split into pairs, one of you will play the part of Banquo, the other a reporter.

Reporter.
You are a journalist interviewing Banquo after the battle and meeting with the witches.
List your questions and interview "Banquo".
What will be your headline?
Write your story.

Banquo.
Decide on how you feel about the battle, the meeting with the witches and the prophecy. Stay in character throughout.

MACBETH CHARACTERS - TWENTY QUESTIONS

How much do you know about the characters in *Macbeth*?

GAME INSTRUCTIONS

Photocopy and cut out the characters on the next page.

Work in pairs, taking turns to hold the characters and ask the questions.

You are allowed just 20 questions to establish the name of the character your partner is holding.

If you guess incorrectly, your opponent receives 50 bonus questions, so be careful!!

The winner is the person who can identify the character with the least questions.

MACBETH CHARACTERS - TWENTY QUESTIONS

Duncan	Malcolm	Donalbain	Macbeth
Macduff	Lenox	Rosse	Banquo
Lady Macbeth	Lady Macduff	Siward	Young Siward
Menteth	Angus	Cathness	Fleance
Murderer 1	Murderer 2	Murderer 3	Scottish Doctor
Witch 1	Witch 2	Witch 3	Son of Macduff

KEY WORDS AND IMAGERY

WORKSHEET 1

In Shakespeare's plays, speeches by his main characters were good opportunities for him to "show off" with language. He created strong images in speeches and soliloquies, using metaphor and simile. Shakespeare used many different literary techniques, but here let's focus on metaphor and simile.

DEFINITIONS:

Soliloquy

This is when a character in a play is alone on the stage and makes a speech where he or she talks about their feelings and concerns. It is a way for the audience to know what a character is thinking and see a side of the character that he or she keeps private. Other characters cannot hear them, only the audience. Think of it as "thinking aloud". Macbeth does this in Act I Scene VII (If it were done when 'tis done, then 'twere well it were done quickly:)

Simile

A simile is a figure of speech where the writer compares two things that seem at first to be nothing like each other. A simile always uses the words 'like' or 'as'.

For example:

"She is **as** beautiful **as** a rose"   "He was so angry that he exploded **like** a volcano"

"You're **as** greedy **as** a pig"   "You were **like** an angel to me"

Metaphor

A metaphor compares two things in a similar way to a simile, except it gives a description to something that at first doesn't seem to fit but is actually saying something about the qualities of what it is describing. Look for the use of 'is' or 'was' and 'are' or 'were' instead of 'like' or 'as'.

For example:

"She **is** a beautiful rose"   "He **was** an exploding volcano!"

"You **are** a greedy pig!"   "You **were** an angel to me"

TASK:

Pick any object in the room. Think of an adjective to describe it. Think of another thing that you could describe with the same adjective. Fill in the gaps below to create a simile. Look at the example first.

The	**sky**	is	**dark**	like	**finest velvet.**
The		is		like	

Now turn it into a metaphor, as in the example. Feel free to expand on it.

The	**cloud is**	**fresh snow in the sky.**
The		

KEY WORDS AND IMAGERY

WORKSHEET 2

Macbeth has a number of soliloquies in the play. The first is in Act I Scene VII and the second, the famous "Is this a dagger" speech in Act II Scene I. Re-read his speeches looking for examples of metaphor and simile.

If possible, underline or highlight them when you find them. Put 'M' or 'S' in the margin next to each one. If you have time, look for other examples of metaphor/simile in the play.
Discuss this as a group. Have you identified them correctly?

TASK:

Look again at the following images from the speeches and from other parts of the play.
Explain what is being said in your own words.

Image	M or S	Meaning
"Ay, in the catalogue ye go for men; As hounds, and greyhounds, mongrels, spaniels, curs, Shoughs, water-rugs, and demi-wolves, are clept All by the name of dogs:"		
"We have scotch'd the snake, not kill'd it:"		
"Then comes my fit again: I had else been perfect; Whole as the marble, founded as the rock, As broad and general as the casing air:"		
"O! full of scorpions is my mind, dear wife!".		
"But screw your courage to the sticking-place, And we'll not fail."		
"The thane of Cawdor lives: why do you dress me In borrow'd robes?"		
"Those he commands move only in command, Nothing in love: now does he feel his title Hang loose about him, like a giant's robe Upon a dwarfish thief."		
"The devil damn thee black, thou cream-faced loon! Where gott'st thou that goose look?"		

SHAKESPEARE'S LANGUAGE

Shakespeare wrote his plays differently from the way plays are written today. Many of the lines spoken by characters are in a form of poetry called **blank verse**. Shakespeare wrote Macbeth using a mixture of blank verse and prose. The parts of the play that look like poetry are in blank verse.

Shakespeare's version of blank verse usually has ten syllables in each line. Each syllable is like a beat of a drum. Try reading the following lines aloud whilst tapping out the beat with your hand:

1	2	3	4	5	6	7	8	9	10
"That	which	hath	made	them	drunk	hath	made	me	bold:"
"The	night	has	been	un-	rul-	y:	where	we	lay,
Our	chim-	neys	were	blown	down;	and,	as	they	say,"

Each pair of syllables is called an **iamb**. In each pair, one syllable is stressed and the other is unstressed. Try reading the above lines aloud to see which syllables are stressed. The style of having blank verse with ten syllables per line is called **iambic pentameter**. This gives the words a rhythm that is a bit musical but also sounds like natural speech. The rhythm made it easier for actors to remember and to say aloud, especially as they had to perform in the open air and they didn't have microphones!

Pronunciation Guide

As you go through the original text of the play, you will notice how some words that usually end in "-ed" are written "-'d" whereas others are written out in full. Shakespeare wrote much of his plays in verse, where the rhythm of the speech formed strings of "iambic pentameters", each line being five pairs of syllables, with the second syllable in each pair being the most dominant in the rhythm. To help with enunciation and voice projection in early theatres, words that ended with "-ed" had that last syllable accented – unless to do so would have spoiled the iambic rhythm, in which case it was spoken just as we say the word today.

This speech by Macbeth: **Accursed be that tongue that tells me so,**
Would have been said as: **Accurse-ed be that tongue that tells me so,**
So that the syllable pairs (five of them in the line) are correct in number and in emphasis (if you say it as "accurs'd" you'll see how the rhythm of the line is destroyed)

Whereas: **And damn'd be him that first cries, "Hold enough!"**
Cannot be pronounced "dam-ned" because to do so would give eleven syllables in the line, and would not allow the right emphasis to be placed on each syllable.

In short, whenever you see a word ending "-ed" it should have its 'e' pronounced to preserve the rhythm of the speech.

SHAKESPEARE'S LANGUAGE

TASKS:

1. Find a speech in the play that is written in blank verse. Divide it into syllables like the example below. Underline the syllables that you think are stressed. Can you explain why particular syllables are stressed?

1	2	3	4	5	6	7	8	9	10
"That	which	hath	made	them	drunk	hath	made	me	bold:"

2. Make up your own conversation or speech using only ten syllables per line. It could be a speech about a topic (e.g. explaining why you think your school should get rid of school uniform) or a conversation where two characters are arguing (e.g. a boy or girl is late home from school and Mum wants an explanation). You could work on your own or in pairs. Try reading it aloud and listen to the rhythm.

3. Look closely at the play.
   Which characters speak in blank verse?
   Which characters speak in prose?
   Why do you think that is?

SHAKESPEARE'S LANGUAGE
(PART TWO)

Shakespeare invented more than 1,000 words,
and rather a lot of new phrases too!

He was by far the most important individual
influence on the way the modern English that
we speak today was developed.

Writers often invent
words, either by creating new
forms of existing words or inventing
new words outright. This is often
because they are unable to find the
exact word they require in the
existing language.

Here are just some of the words:
How many other words can you find that are attributed to Shakespeare?

frugal	accommodation
palmy	aerial
gloomy	amazement
gnarled	apostrophe
hurry	assassination
impartial	auspicious
inauspicious	baseless
indistinguishable	bloody
invulnerable	bump
lapse	castigate
laughable	changeful
lonely	generous
majestic	submerge
misplaced	suspicious
monumental	countless
multitudinous	courtship
obscene	critic
seamy	critical
perusal	dexterously
pious	dishearten
premeditated	dislocate
radiance	dwindle
reliance	eventful
road	exposure
sanctimonious	fitful

SHAKESPEARE'S LANGUAGE
(PART TWO)

And here are some of the phrases:

"All's well that ends well"

"Eaten me out of house and home"

"Method in his madness"

"To thine own self be true"

"Towering passion"

"The course of true love never did run smooth"

"Wild-goose chase"

"Too much of a good thing"

"Neither a borrower nor a lender be"

"Uneasy lies the head that wears a crown"

"In the twinkling of an eye"

TASKS:

1. Can you pick ten of Shakespeare's words, and give their meanings?
2. Pick another five words, and make sentences that include them.
3. Write a paragraph using one of Shakespeare's phrases.
4. Find another phrase coined by Shakespeare that isn't shown here.
5. Make up a word and phrase of your own, giving meanings for both.
6. Find out which plays the above sayings came from.
7. Give an explanation of each saying in your own words.

HOW INSULTING!
THE SHAKESPEARE ABUSE MATRIX

Shakespeare often made up his own words, especially when he wanted to create strong images. Many of these were used by characters to insult each other. Can you work out which words are still used today? Match one word from Column 1 with one word from Column 2 and one from Column 3. Cut them out and shuffle them around. Try different combinations to see who can produce the most offensive insult! Put the word 'thou' (you) at the beginning and you have a sentence.

Words made from putting two words together are called compound words. Can you work out what some of them might mean?

Column 1: **Adjective**	Column 2: **Compound Adjective**	Column 3: **Nouns and Compound Nouns**
artless	base-court	apple-john
bawdy	bat-fowling	baggage
beslubbering	beef-witted	barnacle
bootless	beetle-headed	basket-cockle
burly-boned	boil-brained	bladder
caluminous	brazen-faced	blind-worm
churlish	bunch-back'd	boar-pig
cockered	clapper-clawed	braggart
clouted	clay-brained	bugbear
craven	common-kissing	canker-blossom
cullionly	crook-pated	clotpole
currish	dismal-dreaming	coxcomb
dankish	dizzy-eyed	codpiece
dissembling	doghearted	cur
droning	dread-bolted	death-token
errant	earth-vexing	devil-monk
fawning	elf-skinned	dewberry
fishified	fat-kidneyed	flap-dragon
fobbing	fen-sucked	flax-wench
frothy	flap-mouthed	flirt-gill
fusty	fly-bitten	foot-licker
gleeking	folly-fallen	fustilarian
goatish	fool-born	giglet
gorbellied	full-gorged	gudgeon
impertinent	guts-griping	haggard
infectious	half-faced	harpy
jarring	hasty-witted	hedge-pig
loggerheaded	hedge-born	horn-beast
lumpish	hell-hated	hugger-mugger
mammering	idle-headed	jolt-head
mangled	ill-breeding	lewdster
misbegotten	ill-nurtured	lout
mewling	knotty-pated	malcontent
odiferous	leaden-footed	maggot-pie

Column 1: **Adjective**	Column 2: **Compound Adjective**	Column 3: **Nouns and Compound Nouns**
paunchy	lily-livered	malt-worm
poisonous	malmsey-nosed	mammet
pribbling	milk-livered	measle
puking	motley-minded	minnow
puny	muddy-mettled	miscreant
qualling	onion-eyed	mouldwarp
rampallian	pigeon-liver'd	mumble-news
rank	plume-plucked	nut-hook
reeky	pottle-deep	pigeon-egg
roguish	pox-marked	pignut
ruttish	reeling-ripe	popinjay
saucy	rough-hewn	puttock
spleeny	rude-growing	pumpion
spongy	rump-fed	rascal
surly	scale-sided	ratsbane
tottering	scurvy-valiant	scullion
unmuzzled	shard-borne	scut
unwash'd	sheep-biting	skainsmate
venomed	spur-galled	strumpet
villainous	swag-bellied	toad
warped	tardy-gaited	varlot
wart-necked	tickle-brained	vassal
wayward	toad-spotted	whey-face
weedy	unchin-snouted	wagtail
whoreson	weather-bitten	yoke-devil

GAME:

Divide the class into two. Line up the two halves facing each other, making Line 1 and Line 2. This may be best done outside or in the hall! Take turns to shout out words from the list as follows:

1. The first person in Line 1 calls out a word of his or her choice from Column 1.
2. The first person in Line 2 has to respond with a word starting with the same letter from Column 2.
3. The second person in Line 1 then completes the insult with any word from Column 3.
4. The process starts again with the second person in Line 2, and so on.

Optional extra rule:

Everyone must listen and try to avoid repeating words that have already been called out.

Anyone who repeats a word is 'out' and has to leave the line.

The game continues until only a few people are left or the words have all been used up.

MACBETH SPELLING JUMBLE - ANAGRAMS

The words below are all names of characters or places in the play. Unscramble the letters and write the correct spelling. Don't peek!

Jumbled Spelling	Correct Spelling
RAW COD	
THE FOG IS AN ALM	
BOOM IN WARD	
IE AND NUNS	
DO BANAL IN	
ATE ECH	
CAN FLEE	
FR EROS	
ADD WON CALM	
SEW ITCH	
IS DRAW	

MISSING WORDS

To complete the sentences below, underline the correct word in the box, then write it in the gap.
Be careful – there are some traps in the box!

1.   'Thane' is an old word for _____ _____ or _____ in _____.

2.   "Is this a _____, which I see before me, the _____ toward my hand?"

3.   The first prophecy says that "_____ will become _____ of Cawdor."

4   And that "_____ will become the _____ of kings".

5.   _____ is Banquo's son.

6.   Malcolm and Donalbain are the sons of _____.

7   "I have no spur to _____ the sides of my intent, but only _____ ambition, which o'erleaps itself
        and falls on the other."

8.   The witches have a cat called _____.

9.   The witches are called the _____ _____ in the play.

10.   "_____ _____ comes to Dunsinane" is part of a prophecy.

feudal   stab   prick   forest
kick   prince   Graymalkin
action   witch   lord   vaulting
Macduff   Birnam   Earl
attraction   Malcolm   England
Wood   bloody   Siward   uncle
Thane   mettle   baron   Banquo
Scotland   Harlow   women
weird   quality   knife   qualify
heads   dagger   brother   spear
Macbeth   cape   strong   handle
Fleance   beards   father   King
cap   Duncan   sisters

"_____ _____ comes to Dunsinane"

MACBETH USES WORDS LIKE THIS...

GAME
You will need:
- A game board (opposite page)
- Dice
- A token for each player (below)
- Four players
- A list of words used in the game:

sergeant

prophetic

sleepwalk

merciful

discomfort

fate

repentance

ambition

hail

guilt

convince

consequence

RULES
1. Determine the order of play by rolling the die. The highest number goes first.
2. Each player then rolls the die in turn and then moves his counter that number of spaces forward.
3. If a player lands on a "move back" or "move ahead" space, they do so and then have to complete the instruction for the next space they land on too.
4. If a player lands on a "lose your next turn space", they must stay at this spot and miss their next turn.
5. When the player gets to the Finish line a special rule applies!! The player who is currently in last place can pick any word that they choose from the board. If the player on finish can complete this word correctly, they win. If the player cannot complete the word then they go ALL the way back to START.

Directions when landing on a space with a word:
Say the word and then explain what the word means. If a player is unable to do this, then he moves back to the space he started his turn on.

Tokens:
Use these tokens (one for each player) or create your own.

MACBETH USES WORDS LIKE THIS...

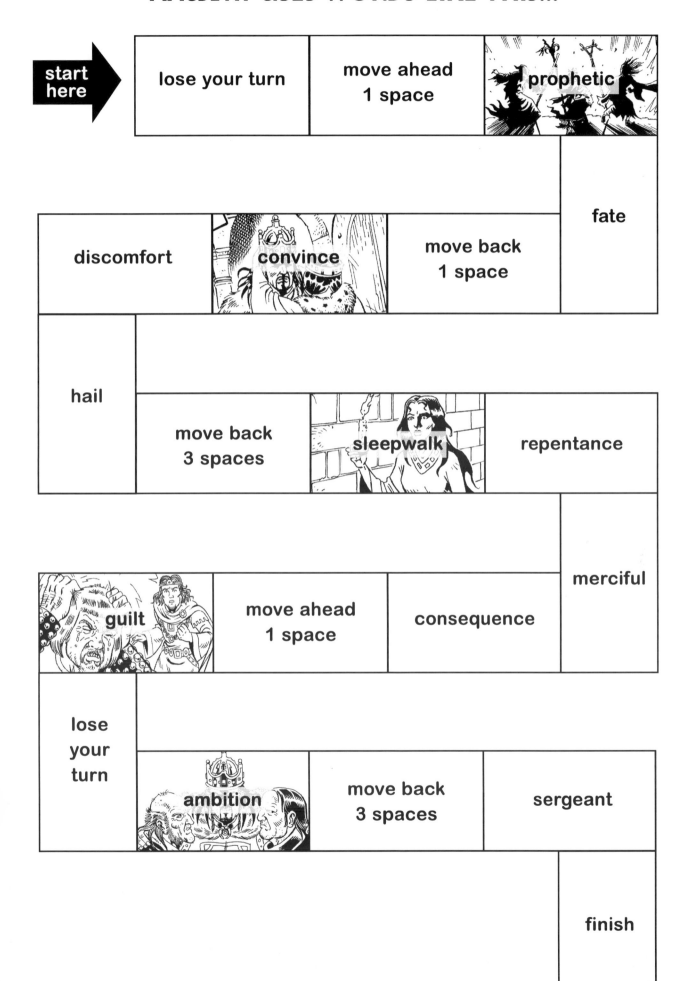

MACBETH WORD SEARCH

Not for beginners!

Find each of the following words.

COUNTENANCE	BEAUTEOUS	POSTERITY	EQUIVOCATOR
DISTINGUISH	BENISON	MULTITUDINOUS	CAROUSING
HIDEOUS	DUNCAN	JOCUND	PREDOMINANCE
SCRUPLES	CONSORT	SOLEMN	PREDECESSOR
NEUTRAL	MOMENTARY	INCARNADINE	REPETITION

```
S  R  O  S  S  E  C  E  D  E  R  P  O  I  S  U  O  R  A  C
N  S  E  L  P  U  R  C  S  Y  R  I  N  D  J  A  C  A  N  D
S  C  R  U  P  L  E  P  R  E  N  I  D  A  N  R  A  C  N  I
C  A  N  S  O  R  T  A  P  R  E  D  O  M  I  N  A  N  C  E
R  E  P  E  T  I  T  I  C  O  U  N  T  E  N  A  N  C  E  E
H  I  Y  C  O  N  S  O  R  T  C  S  A  D  D  P  S  E  I  I
S  O  R  R  E  I  N  C  A  R  N  A  D  I  N  I  U  G  N  S
U  L  T  M  S  T  P  O  S  T  E  R  R  S  I  E  O  N  E  R
O  B  O  O  D  U  N  C  A  N  O  C  E  T  H  L  E  I  U  N
E  M  N  M  E  L  O  S  S  T  D  E  I  I  S  O  T  S  T  A
D  S  A  H  N  N  N  A  H  M  P  U  N  A  S  U  U  R  P
I  P  S  C  I  R  O  C  I  O  O  O  C  G  R  Y  A  O  A  E
H  M  I  L  E  U  O  I  S  D  D  N  O  U  T  T  E  R  L  R
R  T  N  E  N  V  G  U  T  N  U  O  J  I  U  A  B  A  M  O
I  B  E  N  I  S  O  N  U  I  E  T  R  S  E  I  E  C  U  N
I  A  B  U  N  D  E  C  I  T  T  E  I  H  N  S  N  O  C  E
E  U  Q  N  I  A  O  C  U  T  T  E  N  T  I  N  M  R  Q  P
T  E  O  H  C  J  O  A  O  S  S  E  P  P  L  A  I  O  N  E
D  Y  R  E  T  N  E  M  O  M  U  I  I  E  N  U  T  C  A  I
N  A  N  R  D  B  O  P  E  D  M  U  D  N  R  E  M  U  I  T
```

MACBETH WORD SEARCH
PLACES AND NAMES

Some of the following words appear more than once. How many times does each word appear?

SEYTON	SIWARD	LENOX	HECATE
MENTETH	DUNCAN	DONALBAIN	ANGUS
SCONE	FLEANCE	ROSSE	CAWDOR
SCOTLAND	CATHNESS	MACBETH	MACDUFF
MALCOLM	BIRNAM WOOD	DUNSINANE	BANQUO

```
R  N  H  D  N  A  L  T  O  C  S  O  R  E  A
O  A  E  D  O  O  W  M  A  N  R  I  B  C  O
D  C  M  N  N  O  M  S  E  Y  T  O  N  N  S
W  N  L  H  O  A  C  A  W  S  I  W  I  A  N
A  U  O  R  E  C  L  C  C  R  E  A  E  E  X
C  D  C  S  U  C  S  T  D  D  B  Y  S  L  A
H  A  L  C  O  X  A  R  O  L  U  U  T  F  N
T  W  A  O  O  E  A  T  A  C  G  F  U  O  T
E  I  M  N  C  W  L  N  E  N  S  N  F  E  N
T  S  E  E  I  C  O  E  A  B  A  N  Q  U  O
N  L  H  S  T  D  D  U  N  S  I  N  A  N  E
E  E  C  N  A  E  L  F  R  O  S  S  E  Y  T
M  M  A  C  B  E  T  H  N  E  X  O  N  E  L
S  C  O  N  E  C  A  T  H  N  E  S  S  O  R
N  H  I  A  N  N  M  A  A  N  I  A  N  D  S
```

WHAT HAPPENS NEXT?

TASK 1:

Look closely at the pictures on each card in the following pages. In the box, write down what you think is happening in each scene. You need to have read the play first!

Comic Card	WHAT IS HAPPENING? Describe in your own words. Try to explain what is going on in each panel and what characters are saying. Can you remember WHAT HAPPENS NEXT?
CARD 1	
CARD 2	
CARD 3	
CARD 4	

COMIC CARD 1

Macbeth Act II Scene III

COMIC CARD 2

Macbeth Act I Scene VII

COMIC CARD 3

Macbeth Act V Scene 1

COMIC CARD 4

Macbeth Act III Scene III

WHAT HAPPENS NEXT?

TASK 2:

Look again at Comic Card 4. Cut out the blank word balloons below and write in them the words that you think that the characters are saying to each other.

You should:

- Make sure that the 'tail' of the balloon is pointing at the correct character.
- Make sure that the word balloons follow from left to right so that you can follow the conversation easily.
- When you are sure that you have them in the right place, stick the word balloons to the sheet.

You could:

- Write the exact words from the play (this might be difficult to fit in!)
- Write the words in modern English.
- Make up your own words for the characters, but make sure that they are still saying the same sort of thing to each other.
- Write in what the characters are THINKING rather than saying.

There are more word balloons than you need here. You could draw your own if you prefer.

MACBETH QUIZ

Write A, B or C in the Answer column. But beware, there may be more than one correct answer.

No.	Question	Answer
1	The witches are called by a different name in the play. What is it? a. The Wild Sisters b. The Weird Sisters c. The Weird Women	
2.	Who is with Macbeth when he hears the first prophesy? a. Macduff b. Banquo c. He is alone	
3.	In Act I, who are the attacking army? a. England b. Norway c. Rebels	
4.	Who is King of Scotland at the start of the play? a. Malcolm b. Duncan c. Banquo	
5.	What happens to the 'original' Thane of Cawdor in the play? a. He wins the battle b. He dies in battle c. He is executed	
6.	Why? a. He is a traitor b. He is betrayed c. He is fatally wounded	

MACBETH QUIZ

No.	Question	Answer
7	Why was Macduff 'not of woman born'? a. He was adopted b. He was delivered by Caesarean c. He was the child of the witch	
8.	Which Englishman did Macbeth kill at the end of the play? a. Seyton b. The English doctor c. Young Siward	
9.	To which of the characters does Macduff say: "Then yield thee, coward, And live to be the show and gaze o' the time: We'll have thee, as our rarer monsters are, Painted upon a pole, and underwrit, 'Here may you see the tyrant.'" a. Macbeth b. Malcolm c. Lenox	
10.	What was special about Birnam Wood? a. It was named in a witches prophesy b. It moving to Dunsinane foretold that Macbeth would be vanquished. c. It was used as camouflage	
11.	Who kills Macbeth? a. Old Siward b. Macduff c. Rosse	
12.	Whom does Macbeth see sitting in his chair during the banquet? a. Macbeth b. Banquo's ghost c. Duncan's ghost	
	Mark out of 12:	

BOOK REPORT

A book report summarises the content of a book.
Write a book report about *Macbeth*.

Name: _____

Date: _____

Book Title: _____
Author: _____
Artwork: _____
Publisher: _____
Copyright: _____
No of Pages: _____

Characters: Who were the main characters?
_____
_____
_____
_____
_____
_____
_____
_____
_____

Setting: Where and when was the book set?
_____
_____
_____
_____
_____
_____
_____
_____
_____

Plot: What happens in the book?
_____
_____
_____
_____
_____
_____
_____
_____
_____

Did you like or dislike the book? Explain why.
_____
_____
_____
_____
_____
_____
_____
_____
_____
_____
_____
_____
_____
_____
_____

What new words or facts did you learn?
_____
_____
_____
_____
_____
_____
_____
_____
_____
_____
_____
_____
_____
_____

Ending: What happens at the end?
_____
_____
_____
_____
_____

_____
_____
_____
_____
_____

BOOK REVIEW

A book review is more detailed than a book report and assesses the book's strengths and weaknesses. When writing your review of *Macbeth* think about these: Did you find the book interesting?
Did the format of the book help you to understand what was happening?
What was your reaction to the story?
Did you learn anything?
What would you have done differently to William Shakespeare?
Would you recommend this book to others?
Continue on a separate sheet if you need to.

Book Title:	_____
Author:	_____
Artwork:	_____
Publisher:	_____
Copyright:	_____
No of Pages:	_____

Once your book review is finished you could upload it to one of the many book review websites such as:
www.amazon.co.uk   www.whosreadit.com
www.kidsreview.org.uk   www.mrsmad.com
www.cool-reads.co.uk

Book Review:

_____   _____
_____   _____
_____   _____
_____   _____
_____   _____
_____   _____
_____   _____
_____   _____
_____   _____
_____   _____
_____   _____
_____   _____
_____   _____
_____   _____
_____   _____
_____   _____
_____   _____
_____   _____
_____   _____
_____   _____
_____   _____
_____   _____
_____   _____
_____   _____
_____   _____

Name: _____

Date: _____

CHARACTER AND MOTIVATION

Here we explore links and relationships between the key characters, although the mind map can be used in many ways to explore other themes within the play, such as motivation.

TASK:

Draw a mind map linking Macbeth, Duncan, Banquo and Lady Macbeth.

Below is an example of a mind map.

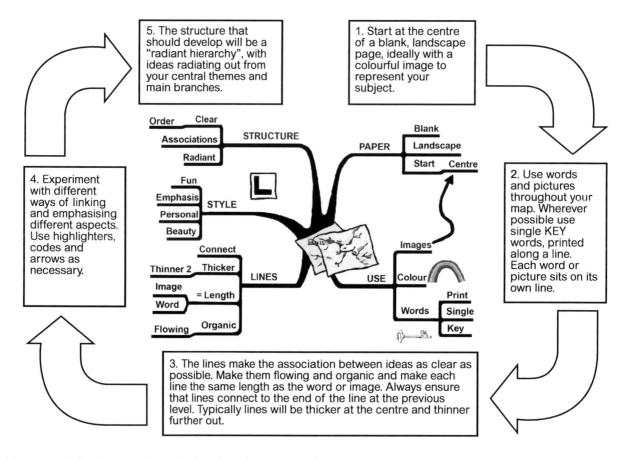

Use one of the images from the book in the centre of the page to start you off.

Now draw lines to each character showing who is related to whom, how they are connected in other ways and any other "joining" threads you can think of.

Explain the connections, using quotes where you can.

MIND MAPPING

GROUP WORK AND DISCUSSION:

1.   In groups, create a mind map of all the words and phrases that you can think of that are to do with loyalty.

2.   Then, divide them into "negative" and "positive" halves. Does every group have the same number of negative or positive terms? Do different groups have different ideas about loyalty?

3.   Use another map to examine the different views people have about war today.

4.   How do you think they differ from the views people had of war in Macbeth's time?

Here is an example of a mind map based on William Shakespeare:

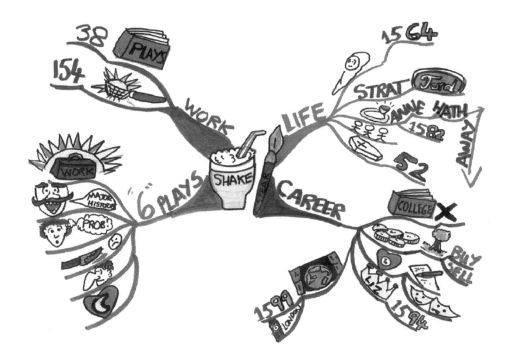

THE TRIAL OF LADY MACBETH

Split the class into two groups. Group 1 is the DEFENCE group. The Defence's job is to argue the case **FOR** Lady Macbeth, that she was innocent of any crime and simply obeying her husband's wishes.

TASK:

Find as much evidence as you can from the play that shows that Lady Macbeth is a good person. You could write this in your own words but also write down as many quotations (the exact words that Shakespeare wrote) that you can find that will help your case. You will need these later as evidence.

Group 2 is the **PROSECUTION** group.
The Prosecution's job is to argue the case **AGAINST** Lady Macbeth, that she was a wicked woman responsible for many crimes.

TASK:

Find as much evidence as you can from the play that shows Lady Macbeth as an evildoer. You could write this in your own words but also write down as many quotations (the exact words that Shakespeare wrote) that you can find that will help your case. You will need these later as evidence.

The Trial:
From the two sides of the class, select students to take on the roles of judge, jury, defence and prosecution lawyers, and witnesses. Witnesses will be characters from the play - dead (as ghosts) or alive.

Characters who will say that she is a bad person will be Prosecution witnesses.
Characters who will say that she is a good woman will be Defence witnesses.

Each set of witnesses will need to work with students from the Prosecution or Defence group to prepare for the trial.

Witnesses need to decide:
	What are they going to say?

Lawyers need to decide:
	What questions will they ask?

Just like a real trial, set up the class so that each lawyer makes a case, then call forward witnesses who are then cross-examined. The jury should make notes as the role-play continues, then have some time to make a decision on their verdict. The judge's job is to keep it all under control, and this role could be taken by the Teacher or a member of the class.

MACBETH – THE INVESTIGATION

You are about to conduct an investigation into the murder of Banquo.

Select students to take the parts of Lady Macbeth, Macbeth, Fleance, the murderers and Macduff.

The rest will become the investigating officers.

The characters should research their parts and remain "in character" throughout the investigation.

The objective is to establish whether Macbeth or Lady Macbeth committed or ordered the murder, either together or acting alone.

Officers, prepare your questions for the characters.

Do you think you can gather enough evidence to send one or both to trial?

Don't forget, quotes from the play will be valuable tools to both sides!

PERFORMING *MACBETH*

TASK:
Divide Macbeth's speech "Is this a dagger which I see before me" in Act II Scene I into whole sentences or phrases.

Each member of the class has one sentence or phrase. Memorise it!

You may need a big space for this part. Outside on a sunny day might be a good idea.

- Practice saying the sentence or phrase in as many different ways as possible:
    - Shout it!
    - Whisper it.
    - Say it in a pleading tone.
    - Sing it!
    - Say it in a persuading tone.
    - Say it quickly!
    - Say it slowly.
    - Say it angrily!
    - Say it as if you are apologising.
    - Say it sarcastically.

- Choose a way to say it that you think fits what Macbeth is saying in that part of the speech.
- Everyone form a circle, standing in the order of the speech. In your circle, decide what you're going to do when you say your line. You could step forward, shake your fist, raise your arms, etc. You decide.
- Go around the circle in order, each person saying his or her sentence in turn.
- You've all performed the speech together!

Remember to use "Shakespearean" pronunciation. For example: -

This speech by Macbeth:

Accursed be that tongue that tells me so,

Would have been said as:

Accurse-ed be that tongue that tells me so,

So that the syllable pairs (five of them in the line) are correct in number and in emphasis (if you say it as "accurs'd" you'll see how the rhythm of the line is destroyed).

Whereas:

And damn'd be him that first cries, "Hold enough!"

cannot be pronounced "dam-ned" because to do so would give eleven syllables in the line, and would not allow the right emphasis to be placed on each syllable.

In short, whenever you see a word ending "-ed" it should have its 'e' pronounced to preserve the rhythm of the speech.

MACBETH - THE SEQUEL

WORKSHEET 1:

Write a sequel to Macbeth!

Split into four groups and each group write your own sequel.

1.   Start with the outline of your story.
      What happens next?
      Who is King?
      What messages could the witches have now?
      For whom?
      Is there a moral to your story?
      Is there a hero?
      Or anti-hero like Macbeth.

2.   Think of using characters from the play - have the ghosts of Macbeth and Lady Macbeth appeared?

3.   Now write your sequel as a play in the style of Shakespeare.

4.   Include a soliloquy. Remember that a soliloquy is when a character is alone on stage and makes a speech. (Look at soliloquies in *Macbeth* again for help and hints)

5.   Try to include similes and metaphors as Shakespeare would.

6.   Use a combination of blank verse and prose.

MACBETH - THE SEQUEL

WORKSHEET 2:

Publicise your play!
Again working in your groups, think about how to get people to come and see your play.

The first thing you will need is a poster.

1. Take a look through film sites, think of theatrical or film posters that have grabbed your attention.

- Is it the words they use?
- Or pictures?
- Or a combination of both?

2. Think of the different fonts/typefaces they use to add emphasis or to begin scene setting.

- Would your sequel have a gothic font perhaps?

- Would you include reviews from critics?

- Should it include a brief synopsis in words, or will you let the pictures tell the story?

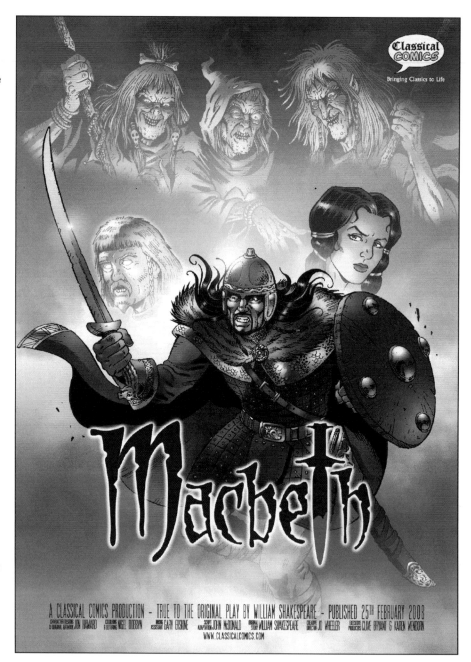

3. Either with art materials or on a computer design and print your poster.

- Remember to include times, dates, admission price (if there is one) and a venue.

You are almost ready to perform your play!

74

MACBETH - THE SEQUEL

Before you perform your play you will need an audience!
You have the script, a stunning poster, the next step is to let everyone know about it.

How will you do that?

Think about ways to reach your potential audience.
- Newspapers?
- Poster sites?
- TV advertising?
These are just a few. How many others can you think of?

A website perhaps?

Or a blog?

TASK

1.   Design your own website to promote the play and your new theatre company.
       There are a number of sites that offer free website hosting that make design simple.

2.   Write your own blog to advertise the play.

MACBETH - THE SEQUEL

Produce your play!
Depending on the facilities you have, remember to include in your script: costumes, backdrops and light/sounds effects.

You may have to improvise.

How can you make the sound of lightning? Galloping horses?
Will you use music?

Can you make backdrops/scenery from materials you have to hand?

Appoint sound/light/scenery technicians from your team. They may have to double as actors too – that happened a lot in Shakespeare's time!

Try the scenes both with and without any effects. Which do you prefer?
Decide as a group how you will present the play to best effect.

REHEARSE!!!

TASKS

1.   Design costumes for your characters. Use collage, computers or paints and pencils.

2.   Plan the sound and lighting effects.

YOU ARE NOW READY TO PERFORM YOUR PLAY!

COLOUR ME IN PAGE 1

COLOUR ME IN PAGE 2

COLOUR ME IN PAGE 3

COLOUR ME IN PAGE 4

COLOUR ME IN PAGE 5

TO BE, OR NOT TO BE – THAT IS THE QUESTION
TEACHERS' VERSION

	True or False?
1. Shakespeare was born in Stratford-upon-Avon in 1564	True
2. His life and times are well documented	False
3. Shakespeare's family were very poor	False
4. He never went to school	False
5. William Shakespeare married Anne Hathaway	True
6. The whole Shakespeare family moved to London in 1587	False
7. Shakespeare's group of actors performed his plays for King James I	True
8. Shakespeare died in London	False
9. Shakespeare was buried in Stratford-upon-Avon in 1616	True
10. Descendants of Shakespeare are still alive today	False

SHAKESPEARE'S SOURCE
TEACHERS' VERSION

"It fortuned as **Macbeth** [Makbeth] and **Banquo** [Banquho] **journeyed** [iournied] towards **Forres** [Fores], where the king then **lay** [laie], they went sporting by the **way** [waie] together without other company **save** [saue] **only** [onelie] **themselves** [themselues], passing thorough the woods and fields, when **suddenly** [suddenlie] in the **middle** [middest] of a **land** [laund], there met them three women in strange and wild **apparel** [apparell], resembling creatures of the elder world, **whom** [whome] when they **attentively** [attentiuelie] beheld, **wondering** [woondering] much at the sight, the first of them **spoke** [spake] and said: All **hail** [haile] **Macbeth** [Makbeth], thane of **Glamis** [Glammis] (for he had **lately** [latelie] entered into that **dignity** [dignitie] and office by the death of his father Sinell). The second of them said: hail [Haile] **Macbeth** [Makbeth] thane of **Cawdor** [Cawder]. But the third said: All **hail** [haile] **Macbeth** [Makbeth] that **hereafter** [heereafter] **shall** [shalt] be king of Scotland. Then **Banquo** [Banquho]: What manner of women (**said** [saith] he) are you, that **seem** [seeme] so little **favourable** [fauourable] **unto** [vnto] me, whereas to my fellow **here** [heere], besides high offices, **you** [ye] **assign** [assigne] also the **kingdom** [kingdome], appointing **forth** [foorth] nothing for me at all? Yes, (**said** [saith] the first of them) we promise greater benefits **unto** [vnto] thee, than **unto** [vnto] him, for he shall **reign** [reigne] in deed, but with an **unlucky** [vnluckie] end: neither shall he **leave** [leaue] **any** [anie] issue behind him to succeed in his place, where **contrarily** [contrarilie] thou in deed **shall** [shalt] not **reign** [reigne] at all, but of thee those shall be borne which shall **govern** [gouern] the **Scottish** [Scotish] **kingdom** [kingdome] by long order of **continual** [continuall] descent. Herewith the foresaid women vanished **immediately** [immediatlie] out of their sight."

GLOBE RESEARCH SHEET 1
TEACHERS' VERSION

QUESTION: Shakespeare's Globe, London	ANSWER:
At Shakespeare's Globe in London, how many standing tickets are available for each performance?	700
Who was the architect for Shakespeare's Globe?	Theo Crosby
And the architect for the original Globe?	Peter Street
Which play was performed at the original Globe in 1599?	Either *Henry V*, *Much Ado About Nothing* or *Julius Ceasar*.
Write down 3 facts about The Globe	Anything that is factual. www.shakespeares-globe.org/
What is the Supporting Wall?	A wall full of etched signatures of people who have donated to the Globe. www.shakespeares-globe.org/supportus/donations/supportingwall/
Because of superstition, what name(s) for the play do actors use instead of *Macbeth*?	The Scottish Play or The Bard's Play.
Name three areas of the new Globe exhibition.	Costume and clothing, Printing and publishing, Music, Re-building the Globe, Special effects
Who was Edward Alleyn?	Leading actor of the Lord Admirals Men at the Rose Theatre.
In which other countries are there replicas of the Globe?	Germany and Italy. (USA on the way!) www.en.wikipedia.org/wiki/globe_theatre
In what year was *Macbeth* first performed?	1611

THE GLOBE
TEACHERS' VERSION

GLOBE THEATRE: Label Descriptions

The Musician's Gallery
Sometimes live music was played here but it was also used for acting as a wall or balcony.

The Lord's Rooms
Here was the best place to sit if you were a lord or lady because everyone could see you – but your view might not be very good!

The Tiring House
An area behind the stage where costumes and props were kept and actors got changed.

The Pillars
There were trunks of oak trees put here to hold up The Heavens. The theatre was meant to be like the universe – divided into Heaven, Earth and Hell.

The Heavens
The canopy over the stage, decorated with signs of the zodiac. There was a space above here from which actors could be lowered through a trapdoor as gods or angels.

The Gentlemen's Rooms
Rich playgoers could sit here on cushions.

The Trapdoor
This led down to Hell! It was a room below the stage from where actors playing ghosts, witches and devils could make their entrance.

The Yard
A thousand Groundlings would stand here to watch the plays. Noisy and smelly!

84

GLOBE RESEARCH SHEET 2
TEACHERS' VERSION

QUESTION:	ANSWER:
The New Globe, New York	
Name 3 of the actors who are supporting the project.	Long list on the home page, left hand side, under "Friends of the New Globe: artists" www.newglobe.org/
Find the names of 3 other actors from the list that you have heard of and name a film play or TV show that they have been in. OR: If you haven't heard of any of them, find out what the 3 actors you have already named have been in.	Hint: Show the students how to type a name into "Google" or a similar search engine and "click through" for information. Alternatively, this could be done as a whole class using an interactive whiteboard connected to the internet. A follow-up activity could be to write a short biography of one of the actors.
One of the actors who supports the project is Zoe Wanamaker. What is her connection to the Globe in London?	Her father was Sam Wanamaker, who started off the whole rebuilding project in London.
BBC	
What BBC TV comedy features Zoe Wanamaker as the mother of a family? Who does she play in the Harry Potter films?	*My Family* is the TV show. Hogwarts teacher Madam Hooch is the Harry Potter character. www.bbc.co.uk Click the TV links or type in "Zoe Wanamaker" into the search box on the home page.
In which *Doctor Who* episode did The Doctor and Martha meet William Shakespeare?	The Shakespeare Code www.bbc.co.uk/doctorwho Click on "episodes" and follow the links.
In that episode, who played William Shakespeare?	Dean Lenox Kelly www.bbc.co.uk/doctorwho/episodes/2007/302.shtml Then click "Fact File" for the cast list.
Write down 3 interesting facts about this episode of *Doctor Who*.	Anything from the "Did You Know?" section of the "Fact File" as above. The episode is available on DVD. Follow-up work could involve view and review of the episode.

WHEN WAS THAT?
TEACHERS' VERSION

Invention	Around in 1590? (Y / N)	Century / date it was invented	Comments
Gunpowder	Y	9th	Invented by the Chinese.
Iron (the material, not the household appliance!)	Y	Natural Element	It wasn't invented – it is a natural element.
Steel	Y	13th Century BC	Although we link Steel with the 1855 Bessemer process for its mass production, the combining of iron and charcoal to make steel was known a very long time ago.
Bronze	Y	c3000 BC	The combining of copper and tin to make a hard-wearing sturdy material was so vital to the development of civilisations that it gave rise to the term "the bronze age".
Aeroplane (powered)	N	20th	The first successful powered aeroplane flight was conducted by the American Wright brothers in 1903.
Trebuchet / Catapult	Y	Pre-Roman	Roman's used Catapults, but their origins are so old it isn't clearly known who invented them or when
Longbow	Y	12th	An English invention, it was used to great effect at the Battle of Agincourt (Henry V).
Motor car (not steam)	N	19th	Credited to Karl Benz (of Mercedes-Benz) although there could have been powered cars anytime since the invention of the internal combustion engine in 1862.
Bicycle	N	19th	Either the 1816 "dandy horse" which was two wheels that you rode upon, or the chain-driven "safety bicycle" of 1885.
Steam engine	N	18th	Although there were earlier examples of steam power, the invention is credited to Thomas Newcomen and his atmospheric engine of 1712, which was used to pump water out of mines.
Purpose-built canals	N	Mid 18th	The canal network was established to transport materials and goods to support the new industries. Before then, natural waterways were used to move things around the country.

WHEN WAS THAT?
TEACHERS' VERSION

Invention	Around in 1590? (Y / N)	Century / date it was invented	Comments
Steam locomotive	N	19th	It is a travesty that the invention is so often credited to George Stephenson and, incredibly, "The Rocket". "The Rocket" wasn't even the first locomotive built by Stephenson! In any case, Richard Trevithick built the first locomotive in 1804, and a later engine gave rides to fee paying passengers around a circular track in Euston Square in 1808 (well before George Stephenson!).
Water pump	Y	c3000 BC	Invented in Mesopotamia, it was a device that used a bucket on a weighted lever that bobbed into the water below and emptied into a higher trough. The Romans used a wheel of buckets to lift water around 500BC, and Archimedes documented the water-screw around 250 BC.
Telescope	N	Early 17th Century	Normally credited to Galileo, it was actually a spectacle maker Hans Lipperhey who invented it in the Netherlands.
Computer	N	19th	Disregarding the abacus and other counting devices, Charles Babbage constructed his mechanical "difference Engine" around 1820. If the definition of a computer is an electronic device, then the World War II code-breaker machines of Bletchley Park must qualify. However, if you want to be really sneaky, the term "computer" was used for a person who calculated weapon firing trajectories, and this role was introduced in the mid 17th century.
The wheel	Y	Pre-historic	We don't know when it was invented!
Telephone	N	19th	Credited to Alexander Graham Bell because of his patent of 1876, although there is evidence of a slightly earlier invention by Antonio Meucci.
Biro / ball-point pen	N	20th	The biro is named after László Biró who patented the ball point pen in 1938 – although there was an unsuccessful similar patent in 1888 made by John J Loud.
Mechanical printing press (to create books and posters)	Y	15th	The first mechanical printing press was the German Gutenberg press of around 1440. The first English printing press was owned and operated by William Caxton. In 1476 he printed copies of Chaucer's Canterbury Tales.

MACBETH - SHAKESPEARE'S STORY
TEACHERS' VERSION

ANSWERS

1. Who is with Macbeth when he meets the witches for the first time?
Banquo.

2. Who are the first three characters to die?
The original Thane of Cawdor, Duncan, his "grooms" or attendants.

3. What is the second prophesy?
All hail, Macbeth! that shalt be king hereafter.

4. Who does Macbeth hire assassins to kill?
Banquo and Fleance.

5. Who appears as a ghost at the feast?
Banquo.

6. Where does Macduff flee?
To England.

7. What is the third prophesy?
Thou shalt get kings, though thou be none:
(To Banquo)

8. What happens to Lady Macbeth?
She dies – offstage – probably suicide.

9. Who kills Macbeth?
Macduff.

10. At the end of the play, who becomes King?
Malcolm.

MACBETH - SHAKESPEARE'S STORY
TEACHERS' VERSION

ANSWERS:

What is the word we use to describe the murder of a King?
Regicide.

In 1597 a King wrote a book about witches. Who was he?
James I/VI.

When was witchcraft made illegal in England?
1563.

What is the name of the witches' cat?
Graymalkin.

How did the people in Tudor times test to find out if someone was a witch?
Floating, jabbing of moles and birthmarks.

How many prophesies did the witches make?
Six.

What were the prophesies?

1.   **All hail, Macbeth! hail to thee, thane of Cawdor!**

2.   **All hail, Macbeth! that shalt be king hereafter.**

3.   **Thou shalt get kings, though thou be none:**

4.   **Macbeth! Macbeth! Macbeth! beware Macduff;**
      Beware the thane of Fife.

5.   **Be bloody, bold, and resolute: laugh to scorn**
      The power of man, for none of woman born
      Shall harm Macbeth.

6.   **Macbeth shall never vanquish'd be, until**
      Great Birnam wood to high Dunsinane hill
      Shall come against him.

FAMILY TREE
TEACHERS' VERSION

Answers to the questions are below.

1. Was Malcolm II related to Macbeth?
Malcolm II was most likely Macbeth's grandfather.

2. Who was Gruoch's first husband?
Gille Coemgáin.

3. What was the name of Gruoch's son?
Lulach.

4. Which royal "house" did Macbeth belong to?
Dunkeld, Alpin or Moray are acceptable.
Discuss with the class why the information differs depending on source.

5. How were Grouch 1 and 2 connected?
Step mother and daughter.

6. Who succeeded Macbeth?
Lulach.

7. Which Malcolm took the throne in 1058?
Malcolm III

Can you research and then draw the family tree of James VI of Scotland (James I of England) showing the unbroken Stuart lineage?

These website links will help.
http://www.undiscoveredscotland.co.uk/usbiography/monarchs.html
http://fmg.ac/Projects/MedLands/SCOTLAND.htm
http://www.electricscotland.com/history/

DUNCAN
TEACHERS' VERSION

ANSWERS:

The answers are **in bold** below.

Act I Scene I

1. Who is Duncan conferring with at the start of the play?
    Malcolm, Donalbain and Lenox, a nobleman.

2. When Duncan says "O valiant cousin! worthy gentleman!" who is he talking about?
    Macbeth.

Act I Scene IV

3. Who has betrayed Duncan?
    The Thane of Cawdor.

4. What does Duncan announce?
    He is making Malcolm his heir.

5. What does Duncan mean by this: -
    "True, worthy Banquo: he is full so valiant
    And in his commendations I am fed;
    It is a banquet to me. Let's after him,
    Whose care is gone before to bid us welcome:
    It is a peerless kinsman."
    "It's true, Banquo, Macbeth really is a great man and it makes me happy to say that.
    Praising him is like a banquet to me.
    Let's get after him.
    He is so conscientious, he's raced on
    ahead to prepare our welcome."

6. What is Macbeth thinking at this time?
    Malcolm could get in his way (to be king).

Act I Scenes VI and VII

7. Who accompanies Duncan to Macbeth's castle?
    Banquo.

8. Do you think Duncan suspects Macbeth?
    No.

9. What does Macbeth mean by this speech?
    "He's here in double trust;
    First, as I am his kinsman and his subject,
    Strong both against the deed; then, as his host,
    Who should against his murderer shut the door,
    Not bear the knife myself."
    That he should be loyal to Duncan.

BANQUO
TEACHERS' VERSION

ANSWERS:

The answers are **in bold** below.

1.　The witches tell Banquo that he will be the father of future kings. How does Banquo's reaction reveal his true character?

"And oftentimes, to win us to our harm,

The instruments of darkness tell us truths;

Win us with honest trifles, to betray's

In deepest consequence"

2.　Banquo expresses doubts about the witches and their prophecies. Give an example of a quote that illustrates this.

"What! can the devil speak true?"

3.　What does Banquo do after Duncan's murder?

He wants to start an investigation.

4.　Does Banquo realise that Macbeth has committed the murder?

He begins to be suspicious and says:-

"Look to the lady: —

And when we have our naked frailties hid,

That suffer in exposure, let us meet,

And question this most bloody piece of work,

To know it further. Fears and scruples shake us:

In the great hand of God I stand; and, thence,

Against the undivulg'd pretence I fight

Of treasonous malice."

And

"Thou hast it now, king, Cawdor, Glamis, all,

As the weird women promis'd, and, I fear,

Thou play'dst most foully for't;"

5.　Why doesn't Banquo accuse Macbeth?

He is suspicious, but a good man and chooses to be loyal to his old friend who is now also his King.

6.　What does Macbeth hope to gain from killing Banquo and Fleance?

To stop Banquo's children inheriting the throne.

7.　Why does Banquo haunt Macbeth? Explain Macbeth's reaction in your own words.

In revenge for the killings.

92

SHAKESPEARE'S LANGUAGE
TEACHERS' VERSION

Shakespeare wrote his plays differently from the way plays are written today. Many of the lines spoken by characters are in a form of poetry called **blank verse**. Shakespeare wrote Macbeth using a mixture of blank verse and prose. The parts of the play that look like poetry are in blank verse.

Shakespeare's version of blank verse usually has ten syllables in each line. Each syllable is like a beat of a drum. Try reading the following lines aloud whilst tapping out the beat with your hand:

1	2	3	4	5	6	7	8	9	10
Me	thought,	I	heard	a	voice	cry,	'Sleep	no	more!'
"The	night	has	been	un-	rul-	y:	where	we	lay,
Our	chim-	neys	were	blown	down;	and,	as	they	say,"

Each pair of syllables is called an **iamb**. In each pair, one syllable is stressed and the other is unstressed. Try reading the above lines aloud to see which syllables are stressed. The style of having blank verse with ten syllables per line is called **iambic pentameter**. This gives the words a rhythm that is a bit musical but also sounds like natural speech. The rhythm made it easier for actors to remember and to say aloud, especially as they had to perform in the open air and they didn't have microphones!

Teachers' note

An iamb is also often called an iambic foot. A good way to demonstrate the stresses to pupils is to imagine a footstep: the heel (stressed syllable) touches the ground first; the sole (unstressed syllable) follows, then it's on to the next step. An active way to experience this is to have the class walk around a large space, reciting the lines in time with their steps. Exaggerate the stresses when saying them aloud. If every syllable is unstressed, the reading sounds mumbled. If every syllable is stressed, it sounds loud and robotic.

TASKS:

Teachers' notes

1. Encourage the pupils to experiment with different readings. Demonstrate how different readings can suggest different meanings

2. For "acting out" their speeches or dialogue, pupils will need lots of space so that they can be as declamatory (i.e. loud) as possible.

3. The characters who speak in blank verse tend to be important characters such as royalty and for important scenes or speeches. Big speeches and soliloquies will always be in blank verse. Shakespeare usually used prose for comic characters (in this case the porter) or for characters of lower social status. Blank verse is generally used to show social status or to elevate the language to sound more important or dramatic. It doesn't lend itself as well to comedy as prose does.

MACBETH SPELLING JUMBLE - ANAGRAMS
TEACHERS' VERSION

Jumbled Spelling	Correct Spelling
RAW COD	CAWDOR
THE FOG IS AN ALM	THANE OF GLAMIS
BOOM IN WARD	BIRNAM WOOD
IE AND NUNS	DUNSINANE
DO BANAL IN	DONALBAIN
ATE ECH	HECATE
CAN FLEE	FLEANCE
FR EROS	FORRES
ADD WON CALM	MACDONWALD
SEW ITCH	WITCHES
IS DRAW	SIWARD

CAN FLEE

MISSING WORDS
TEACHERS' VERSION

The correct words are in **bold**.

1. "Thane" is an old word for **feudal baron** or **Earl** in **Scotland**.

2. "Is this a **dagger**, which I see before me, the **handle** toward my hand?"

3. The first prophecy says that "**Macbeth** will become **Thane** of Cawdor."

4. And that "**Banquo** will become the **father** of kings".

5. **Fleance** is Banquo's son.

6. Malcolm and Donalbain are the sons of **Duncan**.

7. "I have no spur to **prick** the sides of my intent, but only **vaulting** ambition, which o'erleaps itself and falls on the other."

8. The witches have a cat called **Graymalkin**.

9. The witches are called the **weird sisters** in the play.

10. "**Birnam Wood** comes to Dunsinane" is part of a prophecy.

<u>feudal</u> stab <u>prick</u> forest
kick prince <u>Graymalkin</u>
action witch lord <u>vaulting</u>
Macduff <u>Birnam</u> <u>Earl</u>
attraction Malcolm England
<u>Wood</u> bloody Siward uncle
<u>Thane</u> mettle <u>baron</u> <u>Banquo</u>
<u>Scotland</u> Harlow women
<u>weird</u> quality knife qualify
heads <u>dagger</u> brother spear
<u>Macbeth</u> cape strong <u>handle</u>
<u>Fleance</u> beards <u>father</u> King
cap <u>Duncan</u> <u>sisters</u>

"**Birnam Wood** comes to Dunsinane"

MACBETH QUIZ
TEACHERS' VERSION

No.	Question	Answer
1	The witches are called by a different name in the play. What is it?	b. The Weird Sisters
2.	Who is with Macbeth when he hears the first prophesy?	b. Banquo
3.	In Act I, who are the attacking army?	b. Norway c. Rebels
4.	Who is King of Scotland at the start of the play?	b. Duncan
5.	What happens to the "original" Thane of Cawdor in the play?	c. He is executed
6.	Why?	a. He is a traitor
7	Why was Macduff "not of woman born"?	b. He was delivered by Caesarean
8.	Which Englishman did Macbeth kill at the end of the play?	c. Young Siward
9.	To which of the characters does Macduff say: "Then yield thee, coward, And live to be the show and gaze o' the time: We'll have thee, as our rarer monsters are, Painted upon a pole, and underwrit, 'Here may you see the tyrant.'"	a. Macbeth
10.	What was special about Birnam Wood?	a. It was named in a witches prophesy b. It was moving to Dunsinane c. It was used as camouflage
11.	Who kills Macbeth?	b. Macduff
12.	Whom does Macbeth see sitting in his chair during the banquet?	b. Banquo's ghost

MACBETH WORD SEARCH
TEACHERS' VERSION

Solution:

COUNTENANCE	BEAUTEOUS	POSTERITY	EQUIVOCATOR
DISTINGUISH	BENISON	MULTITUDINOUS	CAROUSING
HIDEOUS	DUNCAN	JOCUND	PREDOMINANCE
SCRUPLES	CONSORT	SOLEMN	PREDECESSOR
NEUTRAL	MOMENTARY	INCARNADINE	REPETITION

S R O S S E C E D E R P O I S U O R A C
N S E L P U R C S Y R I N D J A C A N D
S C R U P L E P R E N I D A N R A C N I
C A N S O R T A P R E D O M I N A N C E
R E P E T I T I C O U N T E N A N C E E
H I Y C O N S O R T C S A D D P S E I I
S O R R E I N C A R N A D I N I U G N S
U L T M S T P O S T E R R S I E O N E R
O B O O D U N C A N O C E T H L E I U N
E M N M E L O S S T D E I I S O T S T A
D S A H N N N A H M P U N A S U U R R P
I P S C I R O C I O O O C G R A O A E
H M I L E U O I S D D N O U T T E R L R
R T N E N V G U T N U O J I U A B A M O
I B E N I S O N U I E T R S E I E C U N
I A B U N D E C I T T E I H N S N O C E
E U Q N I A O C U T T E N T I N M R Q P
T E O H C J O A O S S E P P L A I O N E
D Y R E T N E M O M U I I E N U T C A I
N A N R D B O P E D M U D N R E M U I T

MACBETH WORD SEARCH
PLACES AND NAMES
TEACHERS' VERSION

Solution:

SEYTON (2)	SIWARD (1)	LENOX (3)	HECATE (1)
MENTETH (1)	DUNCAN (1)	DONALBAIN (1)	ANGUS (1)
SCONE (3)	FLEANCE (2)	ROSSE (2)	CAWDOR (1)
SCOTLAND (2)	CATHNESS (1)	MACBETH (1)	MACDUFF (1)
MALCOLM (1)	BIRNAM WOOD	DUNSINANE (1)	BANQUO (1)

WHAT HAPPENS NEXT?
TASK 1 - TEACHERS' VERSION

Teachers' Note

This is an activity that is primarily a reading activity disguised as art. The range of scenes covered by the cards home in on some of the key moments, encouraging the pupils to make connections between different parts of the text. A knowledge of the text will be needed to be able to complete the first task "What Happens Next?"

Suggested answers are below.

Comic Card	WHAT IS HAPPENING? Describe in your own words. Try to explain what is going on in each panel and what characters are saying. Can you remember WHAT HAPPENS NEXT?
CARD 1	In **Act II Scene III** Macduff has just discovered King Duncan has been murdered, tells everyone there has been a murder and sounds the alarm for everyone to wake up. **What happens next?** Macbeth murders the guards in an attempt to frame them or the king's murder. The king's sons feel they are in danger and flee. Macbeth is crowned King as prophesised by the witches.
CARD 2	In **Act I Scene VII** While the banquet is held in honour of King Duncan, Macbeth thinks about how he can kill the King and get away with it. But he feels guilty because the King trusts him and is an honest man. **What happens next?** Macbeth thinks about not going through with the murder after all. Lady Macbeth encourages Macbeth by reminding him that he will succeed to the throne once King Duncan is dead.
CARD 3	In **Act V Scene I** Lady Macbeth walks and talks in her sleep watched by her attendant and a Scottish doctor. She rubs her hands as if washing them but cannot get them clean. **What happens next?** The doctor and Lady Macbeth's attendant seem worried for her. It is evident that Lady Macbeth is going mad.
CARD 4	In **Act III Scene III** Banquo and his son Fleance are walking back to the castle. Banquo is attacked by three murderers. Fleance runs for his life. **What happens next?** One of the murderers returns to the King's Palace to tell Macbeth that Fleance has escaped and they have only done half the job they were paid to do. Later at the banquet Banquo's ghost appears to Macbeth.

WHAT HAPPENS NEXT?
TASK 2 - TEACHERS' VERSION

Teachers' Notes

Task 2 extends the activity further for stronger readers. There are a number of ways in which pupils can access this activity. Different ability groups could be given different versions of the task to do:

a.   **Version 1** - Direct pupils towards the relevant pages in the original text of the play. Pupils then copy a key sentence from each piece of dialogue onto a blank word balloon, and stick it on to the sheet next to the character who is speaking. You might prefer to enlarge the artwork to A3 to make this easier. This involves a level of selection rather than simply copying out.

b.   **Version 2** - More able readers could identify the relevant passages as above, but translate the text into modern English before writing it into the word balloons.

c.   **Version 3** - For a bit more fun, the text could be translated into their own more informal language. This could be more "street", but beware! This would need clear teacher guidance and / or intervention to avoid potentially inappropriate language.

The word balloons provided are suggested shapes. Pupils could draw their own in varying shapes and cut them out in order that they fit the page better.

The Comic Script:

Part of the original comic script for this section of the play is on page 102. Included here are the different versions of the dialogue which you could use in part or in whole to help guide the pupils.

FOLLOW-UP TASK:
*   Choose another scene, or part of a scene, from the play.
*   Think about what characters are doing in this part of the scene and what they are saying. Are they angry? Are they happy? Are they walking? What is in the background?
*   Design a comic page showing what is happening in this part of the scene. Decide what you are going to write in each word balloon. Aim to have one or two word balloons in each picture.
*   You could use Shakespeare's original language or write what the characters say in your own words.
*   Either draw your own boxes for the pictures or use the sample grid.

COMIC PAGE GRID

COMIC SCRIPT – FROM ACT III SCENE V

CAPTION	Act Three Scene Five	A Scottish heath…

249. Somewhere far beyond the light of the sun, the three Witches huddle. Strange weather and strange landscapes surround them. They sense the approach of Hecate, the Queen of Darkness and they're frightened.

250. **BIG.** Suddenly she's there! Hecate appears as a triple goddess, with three heads (women's in this frame, all identical, harsh-looking, but not ugly) and three bodies, standing back-to-back. She towers over the three Witches, piercing the gloom with her fierce stare. They cringe and make frightened animal noises.

	QUICK TEXT	PLAIN ENGLISH TEXT	ORIGINAL TEXT
WITCHES (2 & 3)	WHIMPER! WHINE!	WHIMPER! WHINE!	WHIMPER! WHINE!
1ST WITCH	Hecate…you look angry.	Hecate! You look so angry.	Why, how now, Hecate! you look angerly.
HECATE	I am! You dared to meddle with Macbeth In riddles and affairs of death	Have I not reason, chaos that you are, Impertinent and rash? How did you dare To trade and traffic with Macbeth, In riddles, and affairs of death;	Have I not reason, beldams as you are, Saucy, and overbold? How did you dare To trade and traffic with Macbeth, In riddles, and affairs of death;

251. **BIG**ish. The Witches scuttle round Hecate like dogs round their master. Hecate's three heads metamorphose into the heads of a horse, a dog and a boar.

	QUICK TEXT	PLAIN ENGLISH TEXT	ORIGINAL TEXT
HECATE	You did it without me! And now I clearly see That all you've managed to do Is use him as he has used you.	And I, the mistress of your charms, The true instrument of all harms, Was never called to play my part, Or show the glory of our art? And, which is worse, all you have done Was only for a wayward son, Spiteful, and hateful; who, as others do, Wants all he can get and nought for you.	And I, the mistress of your charms, The close contriver of all harms, Was never call'd to bear my part, Or show the glory of our art? And, which is worse, all you have done Hath been but for a wayward son, Spiteful, and wrathful; who, as others do, Loves for his own ends, not for you.

EDUCATIONAL LINKS

MACBETH INTERACTIVE MOTION COMIC:-
www.classicalcomics.com/imacbeth

Macbeth - Interactive Motion Comic breathes new life into Classical Comics' award-winning Shakespeare play. Unlike no motion comic before, this animated graphic novel boasts a choice of three text versions and a full audio soundtrack.

Sit back and watch Shakespeare's most dramatic tragedy unfold, or take control and switch between Original, Plain and Quick Text versions at the click of a button. This innovative software program features professional voice actors, including the talents of Sir Derek Jacobi and Juliet Stevenson in the title roles.

Format: Macbeth Interactive Motion Comic on one DVD-ROM
Price: Single User: £74.99 (+vat) 978-1-907127-90-8
            Site Licence: £149.99 (+vat) 978-1-907127-91-5

FREE TO DOWNLOAD SHAKESPEARE RESOURCES:-
www.classicalcomics.com/ks3

Written to support teachers and students in UK English assessments, here you'll find two sections from each of:
Romeo and Juliet, *The Tempest* (twice as it was tested over two years), *Richard III* and *Much Ado About Nothing*.
The sections themselves are brought to life in comic-book form, using our 3-text-level system of:
Original Text - The full Shakespeare script for the set sections.
Plain Text - The set sections translated into plain English.
Quick Text - With reduced dialogue for rapid, easier reading.
There is also a **No-Text** version, which has empty speech balloons for you to fill in the dialogue.
Each document puts the set sections into the context of the whole play, and there is a teachers' resource booklet with a handful of lesson plans and general activities to help get children involved in these texts.
All documents are Acrobat PDFs and are in line-art for easier handling and printing (they're even ideal for colouring in!)

MAKING COMICS AND GRAPHIC NOVELS:-
National Association of Comic Art Educators
www.teachingcomics.org

One of the primary the goals of NACAE is to assist educational institutions and individual educators interested in establishing a comics art curriculum. Excellent links, and papers on the topic of Comics in the Classroom.   **NACAE**

Scrap Comics
http://escrapbooking.com/projects/scrapcomic/index.htm

"Let's use picture books, sequential art, and comics as tools for teaching critical thinking skills related to sequencing across the curriculum."   **Eduscapes**

Comic Life
www.rm.com/shops/rmshop/Product.aspx?cref=PD1140288

Lets you create comics, beautiful picture albums, how-to's... and more! Can be used on whiteboards with electronic copies of the books in this series.

EDUCATIONAL LINKS

GENERAL GRAPHIC NOVEL SITES:-

Graphic Novel Review Site for Teens

www.noflyingnotights.com

Covers everything from superheroes to historical novels via Manga and cartoons.   **Robin Brenner**

MACBETH WEBSITES:-

On the Trail of the Real Macbeth

www.luath.co.uk/acatalog/On_the_Trail_of_the_Real_Macbeth.html

Look out for *On the Trail of the Real Macbeth, King of Alba.* Essential reading!

Rediscover the Fascinating History of 11th-Century Moray

www.kingmacbeth.com/index.htm

Welcome to 11th-century Moray. Using this web site, you can compare and contrast the fictional and real Macbeth's and learn more about Macbeth's world. And you can meet Macbeth by joining the community of people with an interest in the life and times of this fascinating King. Listen to *Macbeth* or watch an introductory movie. You can also download a leaflet that accompanies a short audio story about one day in August 1040: the day on which Macbeth became King of Alba.

PROMOTING LITERACY IN THE CLASSROOM:-

Graphic Novels for Multiple Literacies

www.readingonline.org/newliteracies/jaal/11-02_column/

In an increasingly visual culture, literacy educators can profit from the use of graphic novels in the classroom, especially for young adults. Educators need not worry that graphic novels discourage text reading. Lavin (1998) even suggested that reading graphic novels might require more complex cognitive skills than the reading of text alone.   **Gretchen E. Schwarz**

The Graphic Classroom

http://graphicclassroom.blogspot.com/

The Graphic Classroom is a resource for teachers and librarians to help them stock high quality, educational-worthy, graphic novels and comics in their classroom or school library.

Graphic novels - engaging readers and encouraging literacy

www.ltscotland.org.uk/literacy/findresources/graphicnovels/index.asp

The showcase resource highlights how graphic novels can be used throughout the curriculum.   **Learning and Teaching Scotland**

Graphic Novels across the curriculum

http://tiny.cc/mJ8CO

The flexibility of the comic medium means that it can be used to tell stories in a simple way, without the reader appearing 'uncool'. However, this same flexibility means that the comic can also tell phenomenally complex stories or explain difficult ideas. This is a medium, rather than a genre, and can be used to create demanding texts across a range of genres.   **Mel Gibson**

Expanding Literacies through Graphic Novels

www.readwritethink.org/lessons/lesson_view.asp?id=1102

Gretchen Schwarz offers a rationale, based on the need for current students to learn multiple literacies, for the use of graphic novels in the high school English class. She highlights several titles, suggests possible classroom strategies, and discusses some of the obstacles teachers may face in adding graphic novels to their curriculum.   **Gretchen E. Schwarz**

EDUCATIONAL LINKS

Eek! Comics in the Classroom!
www.education-world.com/a_curr/profdev/profdev105.shtml

More and more teachers are finding that once-maligned comics, and their big brothers graphic novels, can be effective tools for teaching a multitude of literacy skills to students with a variety of learning needs.   **Education World**

Using Comics and Graphic Novels in the Classroom
www1.ncte.org/store/books/126835.htm?source=gs

As teachers, we're always looking for new ways to help our students engage with texts. James Bucky Carter and the contributors to this collection have found an effective approach: use graphic novels!   **The National Council of Teachers of English (NCTE)**

Getting Graphic! Using graphic novels to promote literacy with pre teens and teens
http://findarticles.com/p/articles/mi_m0PBX/is_4_38/ai_n6123048

Getting Graphic! also tackles the big question: are graphic novels, aka comic books, "junk literature for children," or do they have a "cultural and educational value and belong on the shelves of libraries across the nation"?   **Michele Gorman**

Comics in Education
www.humblecomics.com/comicsedu/

The potency of the picture story is not a matter of modern theory but of anciently established truth. Before man thought in words, he felt in pictures.   **Gene Yang**

Going Graphic - Comics at Work in the Multilingual Classroom
http://college.heinemann.com/shared/onlineresources/E00475/chapter2.pdf

Theory, research, practice, guidelines and resources for using comics and graphic novels in the classroom.   **Stephen Cary**

Graphic Novels and Curriculum Integration
http://members.shaw.ca/yaying/518final/integ.html

"Introducing graphic novels that address history, politics, literature, or social issues in a comic style format into the school library or classroom may begin to help to bridge the gap between what students want and what schools require."   **ESL Teaching in Canada**

Information for Teachers and Teacher-Librarians
www.informationgoddess.ca/Comics&GraphicNovels/teachers&tls.htm

Are you interested in resources for teaching your students:
- more about visual literacy?
- how to interpret the finer point of visual texts?
- how to produce their own comics?   **(Canadian website)**

Comic Books for Young Adults - A Guide for Librarians
http://library.buffalo.edu/libraries/asl/guides/graphicnovels/

"As educators become increasingly aware of the importance of different learning styles, it is clear that comic books can be a powerful tool for reaching visual learners."   **Michael R Lavin**

The Secret Origin of Good Readers
www.night-flight.com/secretorigin/index.html

Discusses how teachers, librarians, retailers, and publishers can work together to bring comic books into the classroom for use as an innovative and motivating cross-curricular teaching tool and a vehicle for promoting reading and literacy.

EDUCATIONAL LINKS

SHAKESPEARE GENERAL INTEREST:-

Shakespeare Magazine

http://shakespearemag.com/intro.asp

You've come to the right place if you teach Shakespeare, talk about Shakespeare, go to Shakespeare productions and films, or just plain love Shakespeare. A Magazine for Teachers and enthusiasts alike.

Shaksper - the Global Electronic Shakespeare Conference

www.shaksper.net/

The international electronic conference for Shakespearean researchers, instructors, students, and those who share their academic interests and concerns.

Shakespeare Birthplace Trust

www.shakespeare.org.uk

The Shakespeare Birthplace Trust is considered the most significant Shakespeare charity in the world. Formed in 1847 with the purchase of Shakespeare's Birthplace, the Trust has since acquired four other houses relating to Shakespeare, for which they care, for the benefit of all.

Mr William Shakespeare and the Internet

http://shakespeare.palomar.edu

"Aims to be an annotated guide to the scholarly Shakespeare resources available on the Internet. Admittedly, some of the resources are not so scholarly, but that's as may be. Usefulness to students (in the broadest sense) is most often the guiding principle. The truly un-scholarly sites are linked on the "Other" Sites page. One very popular feature is a listing of Shakespeare Festivals."

Shakespeare Resource Center

www.bardweb.net

You'll find here collected links from all over the World Wide Web to help you find information on William Shakespeare. There are millions of pages that reference Shakespeare on the Internet. This American site aims to make it a little easier to find your sources.

The Shakespeare Mystery

www.pbs.org/wgbh/pages/frontline/shakespeare/

Who in fact was Shakespeare? The debate continues.

SHAKESPEARE ASSOCIATIONS:-

The British Shakespeare Association

www.britishshakespeare.ws

The BSA was formed in 2003 and is dedicated to supporting people who teach, research and perform Shakespeare's works.

The Shakespeare Society of Japan

www.s-sj.org/english/index.html

The Shakespeare Society of Japan annually publishes a refereed journal, Shakespeare Studies, in English.